Shades
of Blue

ISRAEL BOOKSHOP
PUBLICATIONS

SHOSHANAH KAGAN

Shades of Blue

From Turbulence To Tranquility:
A Real-Life Experience With Postpartum Depression

All names, places, and identifying details have been changed, aside from the names of the professionals in Section Two, in order to protect the privacy of individuals.

Copyright © 2011

ISBN 978-1-60091-177-4

All rights reserved. No part of this book may be reproduced or transmitted in any form or by any means (electronic, photocopying, recording or otherwise) without prior permission of the copyright holder or distributor.

Israel Bookshop Publications
501 Prospect Street
Lakewood, NJ 08701

Tel: (732) 901-3009
Fax: (732) 901-4012
www.israelbookshoppublications.com
info@israelbookshoppublications.com

Printed in the United States of America

Dedicated to Orah –

Thank you for everything.

Table of Contents

Acknowledgements	15
Introduction	17
Chapter 1	19
Chapter 2	30
Chapter 3	39
Chapter 4	48
Chapter 5	58
Chapter 6	67
Chapter 7	76
Chapter 8	82
Chapter 9	91
Chapter 10	98
Chapter 11	105
Chapter 12	113
Land of Acceptance	119
Baruch's Perspective	121
Ask the Professional	131
Ask the Psychologist	133
Ask the Psychiatrist	143
Ask the Nurse Practitioner	157
Ask the OB-GYN	165
Ask the Pediatrician	173
Resources and Contact Information	181

Hope Has a Home.

Abraham J. Twerski, M.D.
Founder and Medical Director Emeritus

The Talmud says, "Whoever saves a single life, it is as if one saved an entire world." *Shades of Blue* can save many worlds.

Shades of Blue is mandatory reading for all women of childbearing age, their husbands, parents, and in-laws. It is also highly recommended for rabbis, doctors, and whoever may be in contact with a postpartum woman.

Abraham J. Twerski, M.D.
Founder, Medical Director Emeritus

RABBI DOVID GOLDWASSER
KHAL BAIS YITZCHOK

הרב דוד גאלדוואסער
מרא דאתרא ד'קהל בית יצחק,
ברוקלין ניו יארק

עש"ק לס' "עזי וזמרת קה ויהי לי לישועה" תש"ע

The birth of a baby is a stressful event that triggers an assortment of compelling emotions, from exhilaration and joy to panic and anxiety. But it can also result in a totally unanticipated feeling of depression.

Postpartum depression, or PPD, is an often misunderstood but well-documented illness that affects approximately 10% of new mothers. Overwhelmed, the new mother feels she has lost all control over her life and sees her world falling apart. Immediate family members cannot understand what is happening to their wife/mother/daughter/sister.

The great Gaon HaRav Moshe Feinstein writes in one of his responsa that postpartum depression can lead to a situation of *pikuach nefesh*. In fact, in one of the standard *tefillos* recited after a woman has given birth there is a petition for the complete physical and mental recuperation of the new mother.

It is for this very reason that Mrs. Shoshana Kagan undertook the monumental task of writing a book on the subject of postpartum depression. The author, brilliantly and sensitively, shares her own personal story and challenges with this experience through the prism of Torah *hashkafah*. I was deeply moved as I read the manuscript; its impact is powerful. The book contains much useful information including feelings and insights from a husband's perspective, rabbinic guidance and responsa, as well as assessments from medical and mental health professionals.

This book is a critical contribution for the Torah world on the topic of the postpartum experience. It is my belief that it will be well received, and hopefully will be found on the bookshelf of every *rov*, *rebbetzin*, doctor and mental health worker. This book will certainly be a tremendous source of comfort to those mothers and their families who currently suffer in silence, perplexed and confused by the despair and melancholy that dominate their home.

May every *mishpacha* in *Klal Yisroel* be able to celebrate their *simchas* בלב שלם.

המצפה לישועה,

Rabbi Dovid Goldwasser

RABBI SIMCHA FEUERMAN, LCSW-R
147-32 69TH ROAD
KEW GARDENS HILLS, NY 11367

718 793-1376
LIC NO. R047809

10 Teves 5770
January 25, 2010

Shoshana Kagan courageously provides us with a frank and emotionally moving memoir of her challenges in recovering from Post Partum Depression. She brings the reader along with her from her early days of joy with her baby, the sudden onset of symptoms and her struggle to understand what is happening to her. She poignantly recounts her journey as she and her husband overcome fear and stigma and turn it into an opportunity for appreciating life's gifts.

This book is an excellent resource and support for mothers and those that love them, who face the challenges of Post Partum Depression.

Rabbi Simcha Feuerman, LCSW-R
President
Nefesh International

SPARKS
Serving Pre & Post natal women & families
with Awareness, Relief, Knowledge and Support

1274-49th Street Suite 427 • Brooklyn NY 11219 • 1.718.2.SPARKS (77-2757) • mail@sparkscenter.org • www.sparkscenter.org

BS"D

December 1, 2009

    As the Executive Director of SPARKS - an organization providing assistance to women and their families suffering from PPD (Postpartum Depression) and other mental health issues, I strongly endorse and recommend "Shades of Blue." This book is a breakthrough in the Orthodox Jewish world, removing the stigma and confusion surrounding PPD and creating a much needed awareness as well as providing practical guidance in alleviating the pain associated with it.

    Postpartum Depression affects the entire family structure, ripping apart marriages, hampering children's growth and leaving a large hole in the lives of many who suffer from it. All this unnecessary heartbreak can be prevented and avoided.

    "Shades of Blue," written as a novel, is a story which women the world over will relate to. Written from the heart straight to the heart, it provides invaluable insight for women and their families. This book will potentially save many lives and strengthen the stability in the home. For the sake of yourself and your loved ones, I encourage you to buy "Shades of Blue."

Sincerely,

Esther Kenigsberg
Esther Kenigsberg
Executive Director

As an organization that has helped hundreds of Lakewood women suffering from postpartum mood disorders, we applaud Shoshanah Kagan for her brave and candid account of her journey. She has written about her battle with Postpartum Depression and the slow path to recovery with astonishing honesty, clarity, and warmth. So much of what the author describes, from her feelings and fears, to the manifestation of the illness, echo the lives and stories of other mothers who have lived with or are struggling with a postpartum mood disorder. In this open and honest memoir, Mrs. Kagan lifts the lid on this often-taboo subject that is still widely misunderstood, giving hope to the countless women who suffer from this debilitating illness.

We believe that this heartfelt book will reassure others that this condition, though serious, is treatable and temporary. Most importantly, readers with PPD will realize that they are not alone in their battle; that there is help and support out there for all mothers and families affected by PPD.

Directors of Yad Rachel Project IMA

Mrs. Tamar Gottlieb   Mrs. Mindy Karmel   Mrs. Toby Tabak

Yad Rachel L'Ima : 1 732 364 4462   IMA@yadrachelNj.org

Acknowledgements

My humble thank you to all who have helped guide me along my journey, and to all who have helped transform my fervent desire to help others into the reality of the book you are holding. I express my deepest gratitude to the following:

My dear husband and soul-mate, Baruch, who was and continues to be the wind beneath my wings. His sensitivity and kindness towards all exemplify the greatness inherent in man. I am truly blessed to have him at my side.

My wonderful children, Avrami, Devorah, Moshe Dovid, and Ezriel. The purity of their souls radiate from within their sparkling eyes, continuously giving me the strength to persevere through the daily vicissitudes of life.

My loving parents and parents-in-law who were open-minded and supportive in my quest to share this personal account with the public. They continue to be a source of wisdom and support to all their children.

My dear sister, Nechama, who helped babysit my (very active!) children while I was busy with the interviewing process. Thank you also for the input and advice given from your perspective as a fellow mother.

Rabbi Feld, Dr. Gupta, and Dr. Kostner for assisting in my recovery and for treating me with empathy, dignity, and respect when I was at such a vulnerable point in my life.

Rabbi Dr. Abraham Twerski, Rabbi Simcha Feuerman, Mrs. Chasya Berger and Mrs. Mindy Karmel, Mrs. Tamar Gottlieb and Mrs. Toby Tabak of Yad Rachel, and Mrs. Esther Kenigsberg, director of SPARKS, for spearheading such wonderful resources for the Jewish community, as well as for all their contributions to this work.

Mr. Mendy Kiwak of SPARKS. for all his valuable input and for helping to move this project along in a timely fashion.

The following healthcare professionals who enthusiastically contributed to this book despite their busy schedules: Rebecca Christopherson, R.N., Dr. Steven Goldberg, Dr. Laura Miller, Dr. Barbara Robinson, and Dr. Mara Tesler Stein. Their medical expertise is praiseworthy, as are their genuine empathy and commitment to helping out those in need.

To the editors and staff at Israel Bookshop for responding to my initial letter and recognizing that a publication of this nature would benefit our community. Thank you for helping me bring this book to fruition.

Thank you to Mrs. Chana Leah Goldman for your listening ear and encouragement.

To my dear friend, Tehila, who encouraged me as one mother to another and helped me to believe in my ability to embark on this project. To my dear friend, Rivky, who is always there when I need her and is a terrific phone pal!

Last and most important of all, I offer my profound gratitude to the Creator of the world for the precious gift of life itself and all the myriads of blessings found within it. Thank You, G-d, for opening my eyes and expanding my soul to appreciate the fact that I am never alone—no matter what life brings. May we all merit living lives of meaning and purpose and bring honor to Your great Name.

Introduction

As I type these words and watch them magically appear on my computer screen, I can hardly believe the unexpected twist on my journey through life, which has led me to author a book. You see, I am not a famous writer, a well-known personality, nor a renowned community activist. I am simply a young wife and mother, who was suddenly thrown, without any prior warning, into the unknown world of emotional illness.

As a result of this experience, I have learned firsthand what it means to be suffering from a malady, which, like most mental and emotional disorders, is often seen as something taboo and shrouded in a veil of secrecy and shame.

Mental health illnesses cover a large range of complex disorders, all of which vary in degree, intensity, and frequency of symptom occurrences, and all of which require different treatments. However, they all have a common thread running through them; that of unparalleled human suffering and anguish that cuts through the very soul of the afflicted. The pain is deep and very real and cannot be truly understood by those fortunate enough to have never experienced it.

My personal experience has been with Postpartum Depression and its related anxiety disorders. It is from the clear perspective of hindsight that I have attempted to write about my struggles, and share with you, dear readers, some of the powerful and humbling lessons I have learned on a very frightening, treacherous, yet ultimately elevating journey.

My reasons for writing this book are twofold. Firstly, it is to spread an awareness of PPD and its related disorders with up-to-date facts and information. But more importantly, it is to write about the unique spiritual distress that consumes a religious mother when she is the one afflicted. How confusing and disorienting it is to have one's lofty, spiritual aspirations unravel before her frightened eyes! Furthermore, the illness itself attacks the very command center of us—our security and trust in G-d Himself. How can one access spiritual fortitude in order to withstand such a terrifying ordeal, if the spiritual fortitude itself is the very point that is under vicious attack?

It is from this unique vantage point, as an Orthodox Jewish wife and mother who has suffered from PPD, that I felt the need to write this book. For although there are many fine literary articles and secular books describing the phenomena of PPD, I feel that for members of the Jewish community, information and comfort can best be obtained from someone who understands and lives their unique way of life. I have humbly tried to fill this role by sharing my story.

And so, dear readers, whether you yourself are seeking guidance as you muddle your way through the dismal tunnel of Postpartum Depression, or you are a family member attempting to understand a loved one's pain, I am writing this book specifically for you. If, as a result of my efforts, even one person's distress will have been alleviated, my goal has been realized.

Chapter One

"Good morning, Mrs. Kagan!" The chipper voice aroused me from my sleep. A tall woman clad in white stood at the foot of my bed. I groggily rubbed my eyes and sat up in bed. For one disoriented moment, I could not place where I was. Then I heard a high-pitched wail, and the answer to where I was and what I was doing there, came rushing back to my consciousness.

"Your little one is hungry and misses her mama," the nurse said with a good-natured chuckle. Then "Nurse Amy," as her name tag stated, proceeded to hand my precious bundle over to me.

"Thank you, Amy," I said, holding my daughter close to me. Her warm skin was still covered with that fuzz that newborns possess. I relished in its silken feel as I smoothed my hand over her quivering body.

"I'll check up on you soon," Amy said in parting as she left the room, her rubber soles squeaking on the polished hospital floor.

As I fed my little daughter, feeling her tense body relax, I gazed down in wonder at the bundle in my arms. Her features were beautiful, unusual for a baby so young. She had a full head of dark hair and a set of wide murky-blue eyes. She, too, intently searched my face, as though deciding what to make of me, the one she would have to rely on in this big, scary new world.

"Don't worry, sweetheart," I whispered gently. "I'll always be here for you and protect you." Then, holding my little girl closer to me, I added emphatically, "I promise!"

I felt a rush of wonderful feelings course through me: the heady feeling of unadulterated joy that the arrival of a new life brings, love that seemed to be overflowing from my heart, and mostly, sheer gratitude to G-d for entrusting this pure soul into my care. I was awed by the realization of His gift to me, and I almost felt engulfed in my feelings of thankfulness.

"Thank You, G-d, for this precious gift," I murmured softly as my baby drifted off into a contented sleep.

After a two-day hospital stay, baby Devorah and I were ready to leave and head back home. "Devorah," I said aloud, rolling the name around my tongue. "Yes, Devorah suits you well," I cooed to my daughter as I struggled to put the pint-sized newborn stretchy on her body. She wailed miserably and tried to fight me with tight-fisted little hands. I thought back to my beloved grandmother after whom we had named the baby. I had been very close to my grandmother and was delighted to be able to honor her memory in this way.

"Are you ready, Shoshanah?" called my husband Baruch. He walked towards the hospital bed, casting his weary eyes on Devorah, who was still screaming indignantly. I looked at her and giggled.

"Isn't she adorable?" I gushed, seemingly oblivious to all the fuss she was making.

Baruch just looked at me with a whatever-you-say look on his face and gave me a tired grin. I knew that he had been up a lot these past few nights with our twenty-month-old son Avrami, who was giving him a run for his money. Avrami was extremely active, and not one to welcome a change in his schedule. This combination left Baruch with his hands full. He'd spent the last two days trying to keep Avrami occupied, shuttling him off to day-care and babysitters, and trying to be with me in the hospital. Both sets of parents lived out of town, and while they felt terrible being so far away and unable to help us out, they told us that they'd only be able to come visit in a few weeks' time, when their work schedules permitted it.

"Your bags are in the car and the infant seat base is strapped in," Baruch said. He took the two gaily-colored "congratulations" balloons swaying in the corner of the room. "I bet Avrami would love this," he said with a laugh, as we left the room together. After the nurse signed us out with what seemed like a hundred papers, we were finally on our way. We exited the hospital's main door and left towards our car with Devorah, who had thankfully quieted down. The movement of her tan and yellow baby carrier seemed to soothe her.

The mid-morning sun shone brightly on us as we walked across the parking lot to our light-blue sedan. "Devorah sure picked a nice time of year to be born," I chirped happily. The sweet spring breeze attacked our senses. As I breathed in May's fresh blossoms and clean air, I felt so alive, so alert. It was as if my feelings matched the spirit of vitality surrounding us. My very being was infused with a heightened sense of self and purpose. I was ready to be the best wife to my special husband and the best mother to Avrami and Devorah. Of course I was tired and overwhelmed by the events of the last few days, but I was so cognizant of the beauty of the world and the goodness of G-d that my primary feeling was that of being high up in the clouds; cloud nine, to be exact!

The next two weeks passed in a haze of endless feedings and sleep-deprived nights. Somehow, we muddled our way through. My eighteen-year-old sister Tova came to visit for a few days, and she proved to be a great help. She took Avrami to day-care each morning and picked him up a few hours later. She spent hours pushing him on the playground swings and delighted him with silly puppet shows. Baruch helped out with the grocery shopping and laundry. His yeshivah's midday break was between 1:30 and 3:15, and he was never left without work to do.

As for me, I was kept busy trying to take care of Devorah. She was a good-natured baby, but she was having a lot of difficulty nursing. This bothered me tremendously until I put it into perspective. After all, I was blessed with an exceptionally kind husband who was very sensitive to my needs. I was also fortunate to have some financial support, so I did not feel the pinch of being on maternity leave from my job for eight weeks.

I was lucky and I knew it with every fiber of my being. In my twenty-four-year-old optimism and innocence, I was confident that it would be smooth sailing for my picture-perfect family. And, in truth, it was like that—until Devorah was about three weeks old. Then things changed, so rapidly and unexpectedly, that every vivid detail is seared into my memory, propelling me back to those balmy spring days of late May.

I remember it like yesterday. I was out walking Devorah in her dark blue stroller, trying to placate her. She had been crying incessantly, and I was feeling tired and overwhelmed. The path leading up to our apartment complex was filled with Cozy Coupes and colorful tricycles, and kids of all ages were outside enjoying the warm weather.

Two or three mothers were chatting amiably on a narrow wooden bench at the side of the path. I smiled at them pleasantly as I passed them by, but did not stop to chat. I was too tired to think clearly and participate in a conversation. Besides, I was fairly new to this complex and had not yet met too many people there. *I'll have plenty of time to socialize soon with them*, I reassured myself.

I continued to wheel Devorah around the bumpy gray pavement, listening to the noisy click-clack of the stroller's wheels. Suddenly, as I rounded the bend near some lilac bushes, I felt strange. Before I could even contemplate what the feeling was and why I was feeling "off," I felt my heart start to race and a sickening feeling in my stomach, as if I had just descended from a huge roller coaster. I clutched Devorah's stroller with shaky hands and walked over to a nearby bench. Sitting down shakily, I tried to collect my racing thoughts.

I knew that what I was experiencing was panic. As a teenager, I had experienced anxiety during stressful times, so I recognized the symptoms. Back then, I had just braced myself and the lurching feelings generally passed quickly. But this time, as I sat on the bench waiting for the anxiety to pass, it was to no avail. My heart beat wildly in my chest, its thump-thump in sync with Devorah's cries. My breathing became quick and shallow, and I felt like I couldn't get in enough air. *Try to relax*, I willed myself, but it was for naught, as my body refused to listen. I quickly got up and began walking home with my baby. The entire pleasant background, which just before had seemed so beautiful and inviting, now became a big blur as I concentrated on one thing only: not passing out.

What am I going to do?! a voice inside of me screamed out. *How am I going to take care of my kids feeling like this?* I forced my wobbly legs up the three flights to our small apartment, holding Devorah, who had mercifully fallen asleep. Walking inside, I tried not to scream. *Just calm down, calm down!* my mind tried to tell my heart. Thankfully, the apartment was empty and I was able to lie down in a quiet environment.

Gradually, I started to relax. My stomach settled somewhat and my breathing becoming quieter. But I was left with a pit in my stomach that had not been there a mere half hour ago, before my walk began. I felt disoriented and very frightened. *Why would this happen to me now?* I questioned myself, trying to analyze what had just happened. *Everything is good... everything is great. I have a great husband and two beautiful children. Why should I be feeling nervous?*

What was going on? What had triggered me to feel so anxious? I began to pick up some of Avrami's loose toys that were scattered around. The mindless task calmed me, and I soon resolved these questions in my mind with a definitive answer: *This was just a fluke. I'll be fine.* But somehow, deep in my heart, I knew the words rang hollow.

I decided not to tell Baruch about my panic attack, because although he was compassionate, I wasn't sure he would under-

Chapter One ❖ *23*

stand. He himself was blessed with a very mellow nature. The words "anxiety" or "nervousness" were not part of his vocabulary; such feelings simply did not register on his radar. Generally speaking, I, too, had a pretty easygoing personality. I did have a tendency to feel nervous at stressful times, but I knew how to control myself and did not project such feelings onto my environment. I'd always been able to keep anxious feelings in check by simply ignoring them and moving forward. No one even knew that I had this tendency, as it had never affected my life in any negative way.

However, I found out soon enough that my previous coping skills would not suffice. As the days went on, I began having more and more panic attacks. They would come and go, always leaving me frazzled and full of intense fear. I tried to ignore them and go on, but they were relentless. My sister had already gone back home, and my workload of taking care of an active twenty-month-old and a fussy three-week-old felt like an insurmountable mountain. It was hard to believe that only a week earlier I had been a typical overtired mother handling things without a problem.

I thought that there could be nothing worse than the panic attacks, but that was before the thoughts came. The thoughts…! What could I tell you about the thoughts? They tortured me, draining me of all joy in life. They were an affront to my identity as a mother, as a wife, as a decent human being. I would be standing on our little porch holding Devorah, when suddenly a bizarre thought would cross my mind: "*It would be so easy to drop the baby over the rail.*" I would physically jump and squeeze my eyes shut. *Stop, stop! Go away!* I'd order the thought, but it would continue to hound me, causing the sickening anxiety to return.

"*Maybe she's not your baby; she could've been switched in the hospital,*" was another common thought. I would try to rationalize that she had had an ID bracelet on her the whole time, and that it was impossible for her not to be my baby, but the thought refused to leave, harassing me to no end.

Or, I would be giving Avrami a bath, watching him splash happily in the water, when suddenly I'd think, *All it takes to drown a child is one long dunk. What if I lose control and do it to Avrami?* I'd begin to tremble in fear as horrific images of my precious son flailing in the bathwater crowded my mind.

The thoughts were worse than the panic. They ate away at my heart and soul. No matter how much I tried to stop them, they'd always spring back like tightly wound coils, mocking me mercilessly. I began to doubt my abilities as a wife and mother, my level of spirituality, and my very sanity. I felt sick to my stomach and full of despair. *What kind of normal person thinks such crazy thoughts?* I would chastise myself. *I must be very sick. Maybe I'm a danger to my baby. Maybe I'm a danger to everyone around me!* Then another side of me would scream back: *But that doesn't make sense; you wouldn't even hurt a fly! Sensitivity and kindness have always been your strong points!* I'd be left feeling dazed, shaken, and confused.

One day, I finally broke down to Baruch. "Baruch," I told him, "I'm not feeling well at all these days." But I didn't elaborate. How could I tell him about my depraved thoughts and strange feelings? He would not understand. He would think I was crazy and be afraid of me. Feeling plagued by fears that, frustratingly, I couldn't even share with my own husband, I began to sob to him, my whole body shaking.

Baruch just stared at me, openmouthed. He didn't know what to make of the situation. I had always been a fun-loving and resilient wife, whose sense of humor smoothed out any rough edges, and here I was now, an emotional wreck. "Shoshanah, it's okay, don't worry," he tried telling me. "You probably just need more sleep. That's all it is."

But I knew that it was more than that. Something was very wrong, although I couldn't explain what it was. I had no idea what was triggering my terrible feelings and obsessive thoughts. All I knew was that I was going downhill fast and did not know how to stop myself.

It was another warm spring day. I was sitting outside with the kids under a shady tree near the little play area. From the distance, I could see toddlers and young children chasing each other, their wide smiles letting everyone know what a wonderful time they were having. My own little Avrami was content with picking up some stones lying around the bench, while Devorah napped peacefully in her stroller.

If only I could be as free as those children, I thought to myself angrily. *Free from the depths of pain that I'm in right now, the obsessive thoughts that torment me, and the dark, dark cloud that has me trapped in its tight grip.* The last two weeks had taken its toll on me, and my emotional health was growing precariously weaker with each sleepless night. I had learned one thing, though, that when I sat in my small closed-in apartment with the kids, I felt even worse. There was a certain degree of relief that I felt when I forced myself to go out. And so, I had taken to sitting outside on the bench under the big maple tree and observing my surroundings.

I thought back to the conversation I'd had with Baruch just that morning. "Shoshanah, I think you should mingle with the other mothers," my concerned husband tried to encourage me. "Maybe then you'll feel better."

Mingle! I thought to myself through the fog that enveloped me. I had forgotten what the word even meant! Since the attacks had started, I had not slept regularly and was physically and emotionally exhausted. Consequently, I was left with no desire whatsoever to socialize. To the contrary, I felt as if a thick piece of clear glass partitioned me off from the rest of the young mothers scattered about the complex. They all seemed full of vigor and spirit as they laughed at their little ones' antics and ran after them energetically.

I felt almost as if I was physically paralyzed—so thick was the density of dark emotion that engulfed me. My legs felt heavy, my movements awkward. Worst of all, my mind felt like it had turned to mush. Confused, fragmented thoughts swirled around in my head, colliding with the ever-present feeling of dread that was gripping me. To break through this all and mingle with others in such a state seemed to be an impossible feat.

But one day, I finally decided to muster up my strength and talk to one of the few friends I had made a few months earlier. Leah and I had both been expecting at the same time, and she had given birth to her son a few weeks before I'd had Devorah.

I wheeled the stroller over to the bench where Leah sat, eyeing her closely. Come to think of it, she looked exhausted, too. Her baby, who was around two months old, whimpered in his stroller as she tried to stick a pacifier into his mouth. "Hi, Leah," I forced myself to say.

"Oh, Shoshanah. Hi! How's it going?" Leah said.

"Okay," I muttered, aware of the subdued note in my voice. I observed Leah's slumped shoulders and pale face. She certainly did not look like her usual energetic and peppy self. *Maybe*, I thought, *I'm not the only new mother who feels this way!*

"Leah, please tell me, do you find it very hard now, you know, after you gave birth?"

Leah looked at me, her almond-shaped brown eyes wide with surprise. "What kind of question is that, Shoshanah? You know it's hard. I'm up at night every two hours nursing Shimon, and he demands to be held or else I don't hear the end of it." She rubbed her ears theatrically. "Sometimes I feel like I'm going deaf!"

I ignored her remark and pressed on urgently, my eyes flashing. "But Leah, I need to know—do you feel, you know, 'off'? Like, you know, tense and stuff, or maybe upset?" I stammered, now ashamed of my remarks.

Leah gave me a strange look. "Sometimes I feel a little edgy," she admitted, "but hey, I look at the big picture and realize Shimon is a blessing, and that puts everything into perspective. Why—are you okay?" she asked me, squinting in the sunlight.

"I'm okay," I lied. "I just feel…a little overwhelmed."

"Oh, come on, Shoshanah," she answered. "You're an optimist.

Just think, soon Devorah will be sleeping better, and everything will look brighter!"

I looked down at my tightly clenched fists, willing myself to be quiet. It was obvious that Leah was not suffering as I was. She was simply tired and overwhelmed. Oh, what I would do to be in her blessed place!

I lay in bed that night thinking about my conversation with Leah. It had left me full of despair. *I am alone in this,* I thought in a daze. *I am stuck in this quicksand of emotions, and I have no way out.* I had not felt like myself for about two weeks now, since that fateful day that the symptoms had started. Devorah was five weeks old. I had no idea how I took care of Avrami and her. I was simply running on autopilot, my maternal instincts taking over. My hands moved automatically, but my thoughts were confused and far away.

Getting out of bed, I passed by a sweet Avrami in his fireman pajamas, and a cherubic Devorah under a soft pink blanket. I headed for the living room couch. I lay down under a light fleece quilt and tried to rest. I was exhausted, every fiber in my body begging for slumber. I knew Devorah would be getting up soon to eat and that my chance to sleep was now. But sleep eluded me.

I stared at a family photo that was hanging on the wall. The picture had been taken at a recent family clebration, and Baruch and I were smiling, holding an adorable Avrami. I was wearing my maternity Sabbath suit, looking fulfilled and ready to welcome a new member into our little family cocoon. Contentment and gratitude flowed from my shining eyes and laughing mouth.

I looked down at my shaking hands. I could only imagine how my bloodshot eyes and drawn face would look if the picture were taken now. *What a terrible mother I am, bringing a new child into such an ugly world,* I thought irrationally. My deepening despair had left me feeling like all the joy in life had vanished, leaving the world cold and cruel. My obsessive thoughts now competed for attention with ever-deepening melancholy ones. *What's the purpose of anything, anyway? We're all going to die eventually,* I thought gloomily.

I felt empty and cold as I huddled, shivering, under the thin blanket. The furniture in the room seemed to dance around in a shadowy haze. The sleep deprivation was taking its toll and I could barely focus. I felt myself begin to nod off, only to be awakened by the familiar feeling of panic welling up within me as I tried in vain to ward off another obtrusive thought.

Again I tried to refocus, and once again my eyelids began to shut on their own accord. But this time it was not a thought that lurched me out of my desperately needed slumber. It was a dream. A dream of a large, sinister-looking, black freight train that was racing forward at full speed. Whistle blowing and wheels clanging, it gathered more and more momentum until there was a sickening thud. The sound of it crashing echoed into the surrounding black atmosphere as it shattered into smithereens. I awoke with a start, gripped with terror. Was I a passenger on this train? Was the train's and my destination one and the same?

Chapter Two

I awoke early the next morning shortly before sunrise, long before anyone else. The house was dark and silent. I lay there, my head reeling and my stomach churning. I felt worse than ever. I knew that I couldn't go on like this much longer. I tried to think coherently. By now, I had pieced together that I was suffering from some type of Postpartum Depression. I was a well-read person and had heard of the term long before my pregnancy, although it had never had any relevance to me.

I got up and walked to the small mahogany bookshelf in the corner of the living room. I took one of my pregnancy-related health books off the shelf and shakily opened up to the page discussing "Postpartum Depression". I stood by the shelf and hesitantly began to read:

"A more serious version of postpartum distress is called Postpartum Depression. It affects about 10% of new mothers. The difference between baby blues and Postpartum Depression lies in the frequency, intensity, and duration of the symptoms. Postpartum Depression can last from two weeks to one year after the birth. A mother may have feelings of anger, confusion, panic, and hopelessness. She may fear that she will hurt the baby or feel as if she's going crazy. Anxiety is one of the major symptoms of PPD.

"The most serious form of postpartum distress is Postpartum Psychosis. The woman may have hallucinations, think about suicide, or try to harm the baby..." (*Your Pregnanacy Week by Week.* by: Dr. Glade B. Curtis and Judith Schuler, MS. 5th Edition. 2004.)

I slammed the book shut with a start, my heart racing. My sleep-deprived mind began running away with itself at a feverish pace. Depression, psychosis, harming the baby... It was as if my fears were being confirmed in print! I headed back to the mauve-colored couch and pulled my thin blanket to my neck, shaking violently. In my mind's eye, a dreadful scene began to materialize.

I was being carried out of my apartment on a narrow stretcher into an ambulance, with all the neighbors standing around and gawking. I was screaming incoherently and the harried medical personnel were trying to calm me. "It's no use," the tall, heavy one said to his dark, wiry partner. "She's crazy; don't bother with her."

My vivid daydream continued on, growing in detail and intensity.

I was sent to a dark, dingy hospital. Around me were strange-looking people holding guns, knives, and other weapons. They all looked deranged, like the kind of people that make you cross the street when you see them from blocks away. I desperately tried to defend myself and scream, "I'm not crazy! Please get me out of here!" But the words stuck in my parched throat.

The scene suddenly shifted to my dear husband, who was standing at a distance and holding our two precious children.

"I can't live with you anymore," my husband intoned in a solemn voice. *"I need my wife to be sane and kind to my children."*

"Please don't divorce me," I cried. *"Please, I beg of you, don't leave me!"*

"Please don't leave me!" I cried again and again, not realizing that by now I was speaking out loud in my living room. I got up and ran to my husband, who was still sleeping peacefully in his bed.

"Baruch, Baruch!" I urgently cried, standing right next to him.

Baruch groggily opened his eyes and looked at me. The faint sunlight just beginning to stream through the window must have highlighted my panic-stricken features, because he immediately sat up with a start.

"What's wrong, Shoshanah? Is Devorah okay?"

"Baruch, Baruch," I sobbed "I c-can't t-take it anymore! I feel so s-s-sick! I don't want to hurt the baby. Please don't divorce me! Please! I'll be a good wife and mother. Please don't let them take me to a h-hospital!" I blubbered on and on, hot tears pouring down my face.

Baruch tried to make sense of the strange scene before him. Being the naturally calm person that he is, he kept his composure and tried to discover the source of my distress. "Shoshanah, what's bothering you?" he asked repeatedly.

I sat down on my bed and tried to relax. "I don't know!" I wailed, my agitated voice waking Devorah. Her high-pitched cry soon joined mine. "I feel so sick. I can't eat, sleep, or even breathe well. My chest feels like it's going to explode. These horrible thoughts and feelings—I can't deal with them anymore!" I cried, throwing my pillow down in frustration.

I covered my eyes and continued to sob, my tears flowing down my face and wetting my clothing. Through the cacophony of my sobs and Devorah's cries, I heard Baruch say in a scared voice, "Shoshanah, you need to see a doctor. They'll help you."

"What?!" I practically screamed back. "No! They'll ship me off to some hospital and tell me that I'm severely disturbed. What will your mother say? What will your sisters say? What will the neighbors say? And most importantly, what will you say?!"

Baruch looked me straight in the eye and answered firmly, "I'll say that I care about you and want you to feel better."

"Baruch, don't lie to me," I said, anger and defensiveness coloring my voice. "You want to get divorced, right? Don't lie," I repeated in a broken voice. "You never thought that you were marrying a sick person who might need to go to a doctor for"— I tripped over the next few words, feeling their heaviness in my mouth but forcing them out anyway—"for mental reasons."

I watched Baruch's face anxiously. Would he continue to tell me that he really cared, or would I find a chink in his armor? But all I saw was a calm yet worried face with dark brown eyes peering at me in concern.

"Listen, Shoshanah," Baruch said. "I don't know why you're feeling this way, but it must have some medical source. I mean, you just gave birth a few weeks ago. Maybe you're anemic or something."

I sat up straight, my heart thumping wildly. "No, Baruch, I'm positive."

"Positive of what?" Baruch asked quizzically.

"I'm p-p-positive," I stammered, "that-that-that I'm going c-c-crazy."

Baruch stared at me in disbelief. "Shoshanah, what has gotten into you?! You are one of the most levelheaded people that I know! How can you even think of such an absurd thing?!"

For a moment I felt relieved. Maybe I *was* overreacting. Maybe I really *was* okay… But suddenly, those intrusive thoughts came rushing back with the force of a hurricane—thoughts of harming my baby, thoughts of losing control in public, thoughts of slipping downward spiritually. I felt that familiar sense of panic and frustration, as I was left defenseless against the horrible thoughts' iron grip on me.

"No levelheaded person has such bizarre thoughts," I choked out to Baruch. "No levelheaded, normal person feels as if they are falling through a deep black hole with no bottom in sight. If this is not a nervous breakdown, then I don't know what is!" I broke out into a fresh bout of sobs, crossing my arms tightly against my chest and shaking back and forth in my frenzy. I saw Baruch's calm demeanor began to crumble, his dark eyes beginning to take on a tinge of fear. I could almost see the thought crossing his mind: *Is it possible that she's right?*

Then he seemed to collect himself. He thought for a moment and then said, "Well, I think we should ask our parents what to do."

"No!" I cried. "Whatever you do, don't do that! Word will spread and the whole extended family will know how inept I am! I don't want to become the next case!" I said vehemently, valiantly trying to hold on to my last shred of self-esteem.

"Well, then, we have to ask a doctor," Baruch said firmly. He got out of bed and began heading for the closet. "I'm getting dressed and praying the morning service at home. I don't feel comfortable leaving you alone right now. After that, we'll go to the doctor." As I began to protest weakly, he added a decisive, "End of discussion!"

Shame erupted in my soul as my inner critic took center stage. *"Making your husband miss synagogue, aren't you?"* its snide voice hissed derisively. *"Not to mention ruining his schedule and disturbing his peace of mind! What a terrible wife you are!"* the voice continued, eating away at my insides. *"Your husband doesn't deserve this heartache."*

"Neither do I!" I tried to answer back the cruel voice. But it was to no avail.

I forced myself to tend to Devorah, who was crying pitifully. Like it or not, it looked like I would be heading for the doctor today to discuss my situation. Part of me recoiled in shame and horror, while another part of me silently hoped against hope that a solution would be found that would get me out of this terrible mess.

Later that morning, our family sat in Dr. Roth's small exam room. "How can I help you?" the doctor asked pleasantly.

Dr. Roth was my internist. My OB-GYN had not been available and I had refused to allow Baruch to call her emergency line. My internist, though, had had an eleven o'clock opening. So here we were, facing the spry and energetic doctor who, although middle-aged, possessed a youthful demeanor.

I barely knew Dr. Roth. In fact, the only time I had gone to him in the past had been for an occasional strep culture. I had always been in good health and was hardly ever sick. I was too tongue-tied to talk, so I nervously looked at Baruch.

Baruch cleared his throat and began: "Dr. Roth, my wife has not been feeling so well since the birth of our daughter about five weeks ago."

I looked down at the wooden floor, my head lowered in shame. Then I snuck a glance at the children lying in the double stroller. Devorah was sleeping and Avrami was absentmindedly sucking on his beloved blue pacifier. *They look so neglected*, I noted to myself distractedly. Avrami's blonde hair was all tousled and Devorah's soft pink stretchy displayed a prominent spit-up stain in the front. I inwardly berated myself, as normally I was a big stickler for not letting my children go around unkempt.

In a haze, I heard Baruch continue speaking. He was describing how I wasn't eating or sleeping well and was experiencing intense anxiety.

"Mrs. Kagan," I heard a kind voice address me. I looked up at Dr. Roth's face. His perceptive gaze looked me over, and I knew instinctively that I couldn't hide the truth from this experienced doctor. "Is there anything else you would like to tell me about your symptoms?"

"No," I whispered softly. "I just want to know what's wrong with me."

"Well," Dr. Roth answered, "what you are actually suffering from is a common postpartum reaction called Postpartum Depression or Postpartum Distress Syndrome. You see," he continued patiently, "your hormonal level is in flux right now due to the pregnancy and birth, and in some people, this causes the symptoms that your husband has been describing. This is fairly common. It affects about 10% of new mothers and tends to run in families. Do you have any relatives who suffered from Postpartum Depression?" Dr. Roth asked.

I shook my head miserably. The only person who came to mind was a distant relative who was seriously mentally disturbed. I never knew exactly what was wrong with her, because everyone in the family spoke about her "condition" in hushed and secretive tones. All that I had surmised was that anyone with any "mental issues" was destined to a miserable, wretched existence. I therefore listened to what Dr. Roth was telling me with great trepidation, ignorantly lumping all emotional and mental illnesses into one category in my mind.

Dr. Roth looked at me pointedly. "Mrs. Kagan, I would suggest that you begin taking an anti-depressant to help you recover. Your symptoms seem to be affecting your daily schedule and are interfering with your life."

I stared at Dr. Roth numbly, trying to absorb his words. "I'm afraid to take medication," I mumbled. "I don't want to be crazy."

"Mrs. Kagan, listen to me," Dr. Roth said emphatically. "Having Postpartum Depression does not mean that you are crazy. It's simply an onset of depressive and anxious symptoms, which come at a vulnerable point of a woman's life. After all, going through pregnancy and childbirth is no easy feat!" He chuckled good-naturedly.

"But Dr. Roth, I read in a book about people who have Postpartum Depression that they hallucinate and experience psychotic symptoms," I said haltingly, my voice filled with fear. "And some even hurt their babies." I shuddered involuntarily as I spoke, watching Dr. Roth's face anxiously. "How do I know that that's not happening to me? And what will I do if—"

"Mrs. Kagan," Dr. Roth interrupted me, looking me straight in the eye. "You are not psychotic. There are severe cases like that, but you would not be sitting here as you are and having this conversation with me if that was, G-d forbid, the story."

I sat hunched in my seat and glanced at Baruch. Was he devastated that his wife was being advised to take an anti-depressant? My anxiety began to mount again as I tried to scrutinize his expression. Through that thick haze of anxiety, I listened to Dr. Roth explain how an anti-depressant worked and how long it would take until it took effect. He also added that because this was not his specialty, he would be referring me to a psychiatrist who deals with postpartum issues. Hearing that, I began to squirm in discomfort.

A psychiatrist! I thought to myself in alarm. *How have I stooped so low that I now need a psychiatrist?! How can I ever go through with such a drastic step?!*

On the way home, Baruch and I were silent. Both of us had our minds full, trying to digest Dr. Roth's words. "Well, what do you think?" Baruch finally asked, his eyes suddenly meeting mine.

I tried to read his expression, searching for a sign of what he would want to hear. I needed his approval now more than ever. I noted that his facial muscles looked tight and his eyes looked very serious. My insecurity reached new heights as I interpreted these signs to mean only one thing: Baruch, my young husband of only two-and-a-half years, was apparently devastated that his wife was being sent to some shrink and being put on pills. Why, he must be sorry that he ever married me!

I took a deep breath and answered him as only a young girl without life's hindsight would. "Baruch," I said in a pseudo-strong voice, "I'm sorry to put you through all of this. Dr. Roth is totally wrong. There is no way that I'm going to some psychiatrist and taking pills. I don't want to be 'damaged goods' at such a young age. No one would ever treat me the same if they ever found out that I took such a step. And besides, don't people on such types of medication look like drugged-up zombies with shaky hands and nervous twitches? I can't stoop so low; I can't!" I stated emphatically, my fists clenched tightly. "Don't worry. I'll be fine."

Baruch looked at me with a mixture of doubt and relief. He spoke haltingly. "Are you sure that you'll be okay, Shoshanah? I mean, I also feel funny about you going to a psychiatrist, but that's what the doctor recommended…" His voice trailed off.

I sensed his discomfort with the whole situation and suddenly, I felt a wave of pity for him wash over me. Poor Baruch. He was just an innocent, young yeshivah guy who was being thrown into this major turmoil—because of me. All he wanted was for his wife to be herself again! I squared my shoulders and willed myself to pull it together.

"Yes, I'm sure, Baruch," I said firmly. With that, I opened my purse, removed the small slip of paper with the name and number of the psychiatrist whom Dr. Roth had referred me to see, and promptly ripped it into shreds. "I will not ruin my life by going through with Dr. Roth's recommendations. Everyone knows that people on medicine aren't 'all there' in the head. I cannot risk being seen in some shrink's office. If I would be spotted, our lives would be ruined, as well as our children's lives!" I cried passionately. "After all, who would want to associate with a 'problematic' family? I cannot and will not take that chance!"

"But Shoshanah, what if you don't feel better?" Baruch asked, his voice suddenly sounding young and worried. The relief on his face had all but dissolved, and now his eyes were dark-brown pools of worry. "I don't think that I will be able to concentrate on my studying if you feel so sick, and how would you take care of the kids?"

I looked over my shoulder at my sweet children who were angelically dozing in their car seats. Wearily, I rubbed my bloodshot eyes with a shaky hand and whispered, "I don't know, I really don't, but it will work out somehow. The worst has got to be over." I tried to sound optimistic.

"Okay," Baruch said nervously, swallowing hard. He pulled our light-blue sedan into our complex's large parking lot, adding, "I just hope that we're making the right decision."

"We are," I heard myself say decisively, even as my anguished heart spoke otherwise. "We most definitely are."

Chapter Three

Once I had made up my mind not to seek help, I tried to get a grip on things and be strong for the sake of my family. But to my deep disappointment, I found myself virtually defenseless against the powerful thoughts and feelings that were engulfing me.

Until this point of my life, I had thought of myself as a naturally empathetic person. Even as a young child, I had always been sensitive to another's distress, the type of person who would try to cheer up others who seemed down. I therefore felt that I had a good understanding of negative emotions and their effect on people.

However, with the onset of my postpartum reaction, I realized that I did not have a clue as to what serious depression and anxiety were and how they could wreak havoc on one's life. For the first time, I recognized that emotional distress is not exaggerated self-pity that sensitive people like to engage in; it's an authentic illness that has the power to completely consume the afflicted person.

The anxiety that gripped me had the force of a lightning bolt. I would literally shake while in the throes of a panic attack. My body would become boiling hot and a cold sweat would begin to form on my forehead. A pervasive sense of doom and danger would wash over me and my muscles would stiffen, awaiting the worst. My senses would become heightened; a whimper from the baby seemed to be a roar, and a weak beam of light appeared to be a blazing ray of blinding sunlight. My heart would begin to beat so rapidly that I'd be afraid that it would pop out of my chest or bring on a heart attack.

The sick feeling in the pit of my stomach cannot be adequately described in words. It would begin as a vague sense of nausea deep within and would rapidly escalate in severity, causing my insides to churn mercilessly. My breath would come in ragged gasps as my heart rate accelerated. I would try to compensate for the lack of oxygen that I felt by breathing in deeply. Inevitably, I would begin to hyperventilate and be left feeling extremely dizzy and disoriented, with an eerie out-of-body sensation permeating my being.

When I would feel the beginnings of an attack, I would usually run to the living room couch and, in a state of terror, quickly lie down. I would literally feel the adrenaline coursing through my body in spurts, causing the symptoms to reassert themselves with each cycle of panic.

The thoughts that would race through my mind only added fuel to the fire, as they were all of a terrifying nature. My most common thoughts during an acute panic attack were that I was going crazy or that I was going to die. Slightly less common but equally devastating, were the thoughts that I would be cast off by my family and be forced to live the rest of my life alone as an abandoned recluse; that my children would be taken from me and would never forgive me for what I had done to them; and that I would inadvertently do something against my religious beliefs.

During these times of intense physical and emotional distress, which the panic attacks brought upon me, these farfetched thoughts were as real to me as the back of my hand. All logical explanations as to why these fears were unfounded flew out the window, together with my sense of security in all that was dear to me.

I remember one particular morning when I was lying in my usual position on the living room couch, shaking violently. I remember thinking through my agony that I never knew that such deep, unfathomable pain existed in this world. I truly understood now how emotionally ill people could feel so desperate that they wished to end it all by taking their own lives.

The way my symptoms manifested themselves was by beginning with unwanted obsessive thoughts and/or a panic attack, which consequently led into intense feelings of depression and despair. I felt that my life was completely out of control, and this frustrated me completely. My idealistic expectation of raising a beautiful spiritual home was disintegrating rapidly before my disbelieving eyes, and I was angry at G-d for doing this to me.

"Why are You doing this?" I would implore to the Heavens above. "I am having children for Your sake, G-d, to raise an upright and devout family and continue the legacy and traditions of our people. Where is the justice in bringing this terrible pain on me? What have I done to deserve this?"

Adding to my misery was the fact that no matter how hard I tried, I was not successful at nursing Devorah. My body simply would not produce enough milk for her, and my baby's cries of hunger would only abate once I complemented the nursing session with a substantial amount of formula.

I tried contacting lactation specialists, but none of these experts could find anything wrong on the surface. I was instructed to eat well, rest, and nurse around the clock in order to encourage milk production. Overall, I was left with the strong message of, "If you really want to nurse, give it your all and you will succeed." But to my dismay, this advice did not work for me. I invested in a hospital-grade pump and diligently pumped every two hours in an attempt to build up my milk supply. I even would set the alarm for the middle of the night, which took out more chunks from the little sleep I was getting. This was in addition to attempting to nurse Devorah regularly with the aid of an SNS (Supplemental Nursing System). Nothing worked. I would only get a half to one ounce of milk each time, not enough for hungry Devorah. I don't think anyone "gave nursing their all" as much as I did, yet I did not succeed.

I wanted to nurse so badly! Whenever I'd manage to sit outside with the other young mothers, it seemed that they all were constantly discussing their nursing schedules, Boppy pillows, and, most significantly, the great satisfaction they felt in bonding with their nursing babies. I felt so isolated in my struggle. The shame I felt when I needed to feed my one-month-old infant a bottle in public was almost tangible. I felt the curious eyes upon me and the unasked question hovering in the air: "How can you feed a newborn that garbage?!" My depression deepened as my body seemingly continued to betray me, granting me only a fraction of the milk I needed to nourish my child. I felt like a complete failure, which only served to exacerbate my anguish and anxiety even more.

I'd often think back to my upbringing, to my high school and seminary days. My whole life so far seemed to have been a training ground for me to reach the stage of life that I was at now. Here was the pinnacle of a religious woman's dream—to embark on raising a family, thus adding another eternal link to the precious chain of her people. I was therefore completely floored by what was happening to me. How was a religious woman, whose primary goals in life revolved around her husband and family, supposed to react when these goals, through no fault of her own, were being decimated as she looked on in horror? What coping mechanisms was she to use if the usual ones in her arsenal, those of prayer and faith, didn't seem to be making a dent?

My teachers never prepared me for this when they spoke about the beauty of a Jewish home, I thought bitterly. I felt confused and distraught, my very identity seemingly at risk.

As the obsessive thoughts and anxiety attacks filled my days and nights, I began slipping into an even deeper sense of despair. Although my case of depression was agitated in nature, unlike the more common, fatigue-filled depression, to me it was no less painful. While the adrenaline pumping through my body prevented me from falling into a physical lethargy, my body was still consumed and dragged down by a spiritual and emotional heaviness. I began to feel emotionally cold, and even worse, spiritually dead. Nothing seemed to matter to me anymore. *If this is what life is about, who needs it?* I'd think miserably to myself.

I began to be plagued by spiritual doubts that bordered on obsessions. My sense of security in my religion had become shaky and seemed to be in danger of dissolving. I felt completely abandoned by G-d, and could not fathom what He wanted from me. First the thoughts had me pondering my identity as a Jewish mother. Before I knew what was happening, though, the thoughts had rapidly snowballed into deeper philosophical questions, questions which left my mind racing and my soul reeling.

Seeds of doubt began to take hold in my tormented mind, harassing me to no end. Every move I made as a religious Jew was subject to this voice inside of me, taunting me about the purposelessness of it. The Sabbath, usually a spiritual highlight of my week, left my soul feeling dead as the voice within mocked all its laws and customs.

The holiday of Shavuos fell out sometime during this period. I remember mechanically going through the motions of preparing for the festive holiday, which celebrates the giving of the Torah, all the while harboring intrusive and tormenting thoughts: Was the Torah really Divine? How could I know beyond the shadow of a doubt? And, for that matter, was there really a G-d after all? Maybe I had just been programmed to believe that, and there really was some credence to evolution. And how was it that so many people believed in other religions; could there be some truth to them? And if G-d did exist, did He really care about me, a tiny speck in the cosmos of the world?

As these blasphemous thoughts crossed my mind against my will, I'd recoil in shock and horror. Then I would feel compelled to answer the thoughts with "proofs". I'd spend hours of time that I did not have, listening to Torah related audio CDs and mp3s and reading heavy philosophical books, all to try gaining the ammunition to fight back at these thoughts.

Chapter Three ❖ *43*

As a religious woman, the sense of shame and guilt that I felt, harboring these unwanted, heretic thoughts which seemed to stick to my brain like glue, caused me a grief so deep, I can't even put it in words. It added to my distress and caused the anxious and depressive feelings to multiply rapidly and escalate in intensity. I felt as if I were living a double life and was terrified that I would "act upon" the thoughts and do something terrible, something that was against my religion. I also assumed that the thoughts were a reflection of my weak spiritual state, and was deathly embarrassed of them. I dared not share these horrible thoughts with anyone, including Baruch.

I tried hard to rekindle a spark within myself. I spent hours praying, saying Psalms, and listening to lectures. Countless times I re-read the journal that I had kept during my idealistic seminary year. Complete with the clearly defined, spiritual goals I had set for myself years earlier, the journal was written with the passion of a young girl on a quest for truth and meaning in life. *Surely reading the lofty words that I myself wrote will help transfer some of the inspiration to me now,* I thought. But all my efforts were for naught. It was as if I had turned into stone, as if my soul was being buried alive, desperately trying to gasp for air, but to no avail.

Additionally, it didn't take long for me to discover that it was useless to try countering the terrible thoughts themselves with "proofs," logic and information. No matter how much I tried, nothing would quiet the thoughts completely, and I was always left with a tiny element of doubt. This uncertainty, which had never bothered me before, succeeded in tearing my insides to shreds and left me feeling like a fraud.

I continued to suffer in solitude, feeling no need for family or friends, even though I'd always been quite an extroverted person. I found myself pacing our small apartment frequently, especially in the still hours of the night when sleep, as usual, eluded me. While my family slept soundly, I would walk from window to window and gaze despondently at the quiet city outside. With every sleepless night, my body became more weakened; my emotional state more precarious. The feeling of having a hard rock in place of my heart grew stronger each day.

One day, while Devorah was napping, I was once again gazing out the window. It was one of my "worse" days, and I was feeling particularly low and hopeless. There didn't seem to be any hope for me. Just then, I spotted Sara, a neighbor of mine who lived down the block from our apartment complex. Sara was handicapped, confined to a wheelchair. She'd been born with a serious spinal problem that made her muscular movements jerky and spastic. Nevertheless, despite her significant physical limitations, seventeen-year-old Sara had a wonderful outlook on life. Her intellect was sharp and her sense of humor endearing. She never seemed to feel sorry for herself, even though she spoke openly about the hardships of living with her grueling challenges. Sara radiated a serenity and joy that drew people to her and, incredibly, she would give others encouragement when they needed it. In short, Sara lived a life of happiness and purpose.

I remember watching Sara alight from the specially designed bus that brought her home from school and feeling astonishingly, irrationally jealous of this young girl who had such a difficult life.

"I would switch places with you any day," I whispered bitterly to her from my perch at the kitchen window. "Your body may be jailed, but your spirit is free. Your soul is alive! You can feel; you can create; you can interact with others in ways that will make a difference in their lives.

"As for me, though," I said, continuing my one-way conversation, "I have been blessed with a set of healthy legs that you can only dream of and a spine as straight and as strong as a cedar tree—but my soul is on fire. Not the passionate fire that lights your soul and spreads its warmth to all those in contact with you. No, the blaze engulfing my soul is a dangerous one, and it is destroying me and those around me. It has already succeeded in extinguishing the light within me. And so I ask you, dear Sara, who has it harder? Of what purpose is my healthy body if my weakened soul cannot generate enough enthusiasm to move my healthy limbs into positive action, to live my life to the fullest degree and fulfill my mission in life appropriately?

"Oh, yes, Sara, I am jealous of you. Physical pain may be devastating, but at least you can use your sharp intellect and spiritual strengths to fortify you and keep you going. And the real you—your essence—is alive and as healthy as ever. But *my* essence is being targeted in this insidious battle which I don't seem to be winning. I can't properly fight against the illness, because the tools of logic and faith that I need are under attack. I am therefore defenseless, completely defenseless," I concluded in misery.

The relentless feelings of panic, obsessive thoughts, and apathy continued. I truly felt that there was no way out of my predicament. Yet despite the deep pain I was experiencing, I still refused to contemplate going for help. Looking back, I am amazed at the power of the stigma surrounding mental and emotional illness in society. The shame it created was, incredibly, strong enough to overpower the horrifying and debilitating emotions that were destroying me!

The one positive aspect that began to emerge from this dreadful time in my life was the feeling of humility that I gained. No longer did I feel smug and complacent as a contributing member of my family and the general community. Now I truly understood the axiom, "But for the grace of G-d go I." For I saw, as I had never seen before, how truly dependent we are on G-d for everything—including our mental health.

For the first time in my life, I began to notice the seriously mentally impaired members of society around me. I would note the strange, quirky, and often lonely people wandering around the neighborhood, their movements odd and their eyes glazed over. It was obvious to any perceptive onlooker that these people were suffering from serious mental-health issues.

Even in my horrible state, I knew that the mental anguish they were suffering was of an entirely different league, to the extent that they could not function normally. Most of them could not have families or hold down jobs. Many were dependent on others for their everyday needs.

When I'd see such people, I'd become consumed with terror, as I was petrified of "joining their camp," but at the same time, I'd look at them and become filled with tremendous compassion. For the first time in my life, I was able to look past these unfortunate people's strange behaviors, and I was able to see human beings suffering raw anguish. These members of society had been afflicted through no fault of their own, by a higher, Divine court, for reasons known only to G-d Himself.

The slight, middle-aged lady who would occasionally talk to herself aloud; the wild teenage boy whose incoherent speech and odd movements scared people away from him; the wrinkled old man who averted his gaze from everyone and walked around the neighborhood carrying all his belongings…I suddenly saw through these people's sorry-looking external qualities and glimpsed their suffering souls within.

The rock in my chest eroded just a bit as I watched these harmless neighborhood people wallowing alone in their misery; alone in the world of the seriously mentally impaired, where few were brave enough to enter and lend a loving smile and helping hand. I felt as if my blinders had been torn off and I had a glimpse into a world where relentless pain is a daily companion. From that point and on, I knew that it would never again be possible for me to brush aside such people's pain with a callous shrug. My venture into this world of mental anguish and emotional pain had sensitized me as no other lesson ever could.

And so the days and nights dragged on, adding more and more links to my long chain of terror. All the while, I continued to play the ridiculous game of Make-Believe, pretending that I was fine while in truth I was shriveling up inside.

Chapter Four

In the midst of all my agony, one day I received a phone call from my mother.

"Guess what, Shoshanah?" my mother said happily. "Daddy just told me that he could take off from work for a couple days next week, so we could finally come and see you and the baby!"

I swallowed hard. Normally, a visit from my parents, whom I saw so infrequently, would have elicited a thrill of excitement within me. Now, though, it filled me with uneasiness and a sense of foreboding. How would I handle myself with my parents there? Would my mother pick up on my horrible state of mind and begin questioning me about it?

When my parents entered our apartment, Avrami ran over to them, shouting, "Bub-by! Zai-dy!" I was grateful for his carefree glee and let him interact with my parents while I went to get Devorah from the bedroom.

Shakily, I picked up the baby and brought her out to meet my parents. Swaddled tightly in a fuzzy yellow blanket that was decorated with miniature baby ducklings, Devorah looked absolutely adorable, and my parents took to her immediately, cooing to her and kissing her excitedly. We are a small family, and every grandchild who is born is a cause of great excitement and fanfare for everyone.

For the next few hours, my parents were completely preoccupied with the children. They unpacked toys for Avrami and cute little stretchies and onesies for Devorah. My feeble-sounding thanks for the gifts were fortunately drowned out by Avrami's excited yelling and shouting. He wasn't used to receiving so many new toys at once, and was clearly reveling in it!

I kept wondering if my parents noticed how horrible I was feeling. Were my churning emotions being reflected on the outside by my facial expressions and body language? Just when I had concluded that I must be emotionally opaque, since no one had mentioned anything, my mother turned to me and softly asked, "What's wrong, Shoshanah?"

I glanced at my mother and for a split second, my gaze met hers. Then I quickly looked away, my eyes darting nervously around the room. I wanted so badly to run straight into my mother's arms and blurt out all my problems to her, get everything off my chest and be able to cry on her shoulder—but I couldn't bring myself to do it. My mother had not had an easy year. Her mother had passed away after a long and debilitating illness, and various other personal struggles had recently cropped up in my mother's life, as well. My father, too, was under a great deal of pressure, having experienced several financial setbacks in his business lately. I knew that the birth of Devorah had been a great boost for both of my parents, and had filled their hearts with much-needed joy. How could I now mar their happiness?

So, I feigned a light tone and stoically answered, "Nothing really, Ma. I'm just very tired with taking care of the kids and all. I'll be fine."

Mentally, I gave myself a wry pat on the back. I felt like a real martyr, foregoing my entitled sense of catharsis that I could have easily attained by pouring out my heart to my mother. I was valiantly holding back my fears and frustrations, so as not to upset my parents at a difficult period in their lives. What a wonderful daughter I was!

Inwardly, though, I knew that what I was doing was not healthy, nor was it the right thing to do at this point. Now was not the time to play the role of a martyr. Now was the time to get myself much-needed help and direction, and if I truly felt that my parents were not in the right state to help me at this time, I should have at least turned to someone else. But, as usual, my mind was too foggy, confused, and exhausted to give proper thought to this decision of mine of continuing to play "Make-Believe". All I could feel was an overwhelming sense of responsibility not to let my parents down, to make sure to protect them from the horror in which I found myself enmeshed.

My mother, for her part, did not quite believe me. Throughout the three-day visit, she kept asking me what was wrong. She was concerned that I looked so exhausted and listless, and wryly commented that I had lost my ability to crack a good joke, something for which I was famous in my family.

"What's bothering you, Shoshanah?" she repeatedly asked me. "What's bothering you?"

At one point, my defenses faltered and I finally confided in her. I tearfully explained that I felt very off-kilter and suspected that I was suffering from Postpartum Depression. My mother seemed relieved that I was finally opening up to her, but did not quite know how to proceed after that.

"Shoshanah," she said, valiantly trying to reassure me, "you should know that it's very normal to feel 'off' after childbirth. I remember that some of my friends experienced this, too. What I think you need to do in order to get back to yourself is to take things a lot easier. Get more babysitting help and more cleaning help so you won't have to work as hard. You'll see—you'll feel so much less stress, and you'll start getting your strength back." Then, as an added incentive to try to convince me, she added, "I'll speak to Daddy and we'll help pay for it."

She then had a long discussion with Baruch about how much more I needed his assistance now.

I realized from the conversation that my mother did not recognize the extent of my agony. I was beyond "getting more help". All the babysitting in the world could not help me fall asleep or stop the panic attacks. And as far as Baruch helping me out more, I knew that I had been blessed with a very special husband who was already helping me a great deal, and whom I already knew I could always count on.

After this conversation with my mother, I had a new thing to worry about: the fact that I had let my parents down, that my "perfect daughter status" was at risk. As ridiculous as it may sound, long ago I had unofficially crowned myself with this title, and for good reason, at least to my mind. I had always been a good daughter, going out of my way to please my parents and spare them any discomfort. I prided myself with this "status", but after my disclosure to my mother, although I was still truly assured of my parents' love for me, my self-esteem took another rapid plummet. No longer was I the perfect daughter who never gave her parents a thing to worry about.

I knew my mother well. Right away, I could tell that she was uncomfortable with the whole topic of PPD, and that's why she just wanted to "wish away" the entire issue with some pat advice. Indeed, now that she had offered to get me extra help, she actually seemed to believe that the problem was over!

"Shoshanah, you'll be fine," she kept telling me. "Once you have the extra help, and you don't focus so much on how you feel, you'll see—this will all go away." Of course, I knew that her advice was not for someone suffering at my level. Perhaps it could have worked for a new mother who had some slight "baby blues"—but not for someone suffering with the degree of depression and anxiety that I had.

The horrible feeling of not being properly understood added salt to my wounds, intensifying my misery and causing me to clamp my mouth shut again. *I will not try again to unburden myself and get help for my problem!* I thought fiercely to myself.

The intellectual side of me well understood that my mother was from a generation where topics such as PPD were taboo and simply not discussed. In the post-Holocaust generation, people were focused on rebuilding and did not have the time, energy, or know-how with which to analyze their inner selves, for better or for worse. People from that generation had gone through enough and, understandably, tended to sweep any additional areas of suffering under the carpet. My parents had grown up in that generation and were very much products of it. As such, although my kindhearted mother truly felt bad for me and wanted to help alleviate my distressing symptoms, the only tool she could suggest was the escape method that she had seen employed as a child of her generation, namely: Don't talk about it—don't think about it—just move on.

But my emotional side was crying out in agonizing pain! Why couldn't she understand? I could not "just move on" and not dwell on my symptoms. I *was* my symptoms. My entire being had morphed into an anxiety-ridden and depressed person. This was not like a physical ailment where the person remains the same person, but just has some pain in his body. My whole personality had changed. My very essence was under attack. The lighthearted, fun, and people-loving part of me had all but shattered under the heavy black weight, which pressed upon me during the day and choked me in the dark hours of the night.

Mommy, of course I want to "escape" my misery! But where could I escape to? Wherever I go, the depression follows me! How does one escape if an extra cleaning lady just won't do the trick?

About two weeks after my parents' visit, we were scheduled to visit Baruch's parents who lived a plane ride away in a small community in Canada. My husband's first cousin was getting married there, and we had long ago obtained tickets to fly in and attend the wedding, while simultaneously having the opportunity to visit my in-laws.

I felt sick to my stomach at the thought of the plane ride and of meeting my in-laws in my weakened state. Although I truly did not feel up to the trip, both emotionally and physically, it never entered my mind to cancel the trip. After all, this was Baruch's first cousin's wedding! My husband's family is extremely tight-knit, with every cousin being like a sibling. Ever the perpetual people-pleaser, I didn't want to hurt anyone's feelings by canceling the trip. I also knew that my husband's parents, who had no idea of what was going on with me, were eager to see the new baby and Avrami, and I didn't want to let them down, either.

The thought of meeting face-to-face with my in-laws, especially my mother-in-law, caused fresh waves of intense anxiety to shoot through me. My mother-in-law is one of the kindest and nicest people one could possibly know. She is a very generous and accepting woman, who raised a beautiful family and worked hard on instilling good character traits in her children. But after only two-and-a-half years of marriage, I was still insecure and worried about what she thought of me, her daughter-in-law.

To a newly-married young woman, a mother-in-law is universally—although usually erroneously—viewed as a formidable force; a force of immeasurable strength that has the power to wreak havoc in her daughter-in-law's life. And typical of my age and status in life, I was, quite frankly, scared of my mother-in-law. While with my own mother I knew that I could always bare my soul and still be assured of her love, I did not yet feel that way with my mother-in-law. In my young eyes, breaking down in front of my mother-in-law would lead her to reject me and regret her beloved son's marriage to me. I just could not bear the thought of this disapproval. My head swam at the thought, and my stomach churned incessantly. My anxiety level increased manifold as the day of our departure loomed closer, leaving me shaking even more under my blanket on the couch each day.

And so it was that with great trepidation, I boarded the American Airlines jet with my family. I was so overwhelmed with anxiety that the other passengers on the plane appeared like Martians to me, their features bizarre and distorted to my unfocused eyes. I clamped my mouth shut to keep from screaming, as my inner voice let me know in stark terms that insanity was just around the corner. I held Devorah tightly as we ascended into the sky, and looked out the window at the puffy white clouds surrounding us. I desperately wished for the plane to crash, so that I'd be taken away from all this pain.

We landed a few hours later and were greeted in the bustling airport by Baruch's parents. I could barely look at my mother-in-law, so great was my apprehension. With the help of my overactive imagination, I had succeeded in building my mother-in-law up in my mind into beast of mammoth proportions, a beast who possessed supernatural powers and would use them to zap down any happily married couple where the wife was suffering from an emotional ailment.

My unsuspecting and innocent in-laws greeted us with great joy and cooed over the new baby. I somehow gave them a plastic smile and went through all the appropriate motions. We were then driven back to my husband's childhood home, a large white colonial complete with a picturesque and carefully tended garden in the front. As I realized that my mother-in-law did not seem to suspect anything, I was able to relax somewhat and was even able to sit down and drink a cup of orange juice with her upon our arrival at the house. We chit-chatted for a little while, and then I excused myself, saying that I needed to put the baby in for a nap.

Moments later, I found myself in the spacious pastel-blue bedroom that had been lovingly prepared for our visit. A cozy little bassinet was waiting for my tired baby, and I gently put her inside. Then I lay down on my bed and watched the ceiling fan turn methodically, calmed a bit more by its continuous motion.

Okay, I told myself. *So you managed to cover things up until now. Just continue with what you've been doing, and this visit will soon be over. But whatever you do, don't disclose any of your feelings or portray any confusion—under no circumstances! Baruch's mother would disown you if she knew that you were feeling depressed. You know how protective she is of her precious Baruch.*

I then pinched my cheeks to give myself some color and pasted my rubber smile back on my face. I smoothed out my skirt and headed to the stairs to continue acting in the biggest charade of my life.

However, I soon found out that charades don't last long, especially not after continuous nights of insomnia. As horrible as things had been for me in my own home, in this "dangerous" territory, it was ten times worse. My mind simply refused to settle, and with my racing thoughts and bouts of violent shaking, it was impossible for me to fall asleep. I would toss and turn in bed, crying muffled sobs into my soft pillow, all the while dreading the thought of morning's arrival. I couldn't wait for this wretched visit to be over.

Sure enough, it didn't take long for my in-laws to approach my husband and ask him why I seemed so aloof and withdrawn. He answered with our familiar mantra. "Shoshanah's tired; that's all." When pressed a bit more, he finally admitted that I was not feeling well and needed more time to recuperate after the birth of Devorah. My in-laws tried to ask Baruch for more details, but my loyal husband would reveal no more, instead just giving them some sketchy and vague responses. Poor Baruch was also worried about alarming his parents and causing them to over-react, which in turn, we both knew, would just make my symptoms become even worse.

Looking back, I realize now how immature and naive we were. Here we were, a very young couple, with two little babies depending on us, trying to grapple with a very real problem on our own. We did not have life's experience behind us and sorely needed some guidance. Yes, had my in-laws have been alerted to the severity of the circumstances, they may have become overprotective and overly involved. However, our decision to suffer in a dangerous silence was neither any wiser nor healthier.

When my husband told me about the little exchange that he'd had with his parents, I flew into an uncharacteristic rage. "How could you?" I sputtered angrily, clenching my fists. "You know what's next," I continued, spitting out my words rapidly. "They interfere and break up our marriage. What are our poor children going to do with divorced parents?"

I was being completely unreasonable and histrionic, yet at the time, I honestly did not realize that. The anxiety that I was suffering from had caused me to think in suspicious and paranoid terms. I had zeroed in on my in-laws' slight tendency to be overprotective of their children and had magnified it into a pathological illness that caused parents to intentionally break up a child's marriage in order to protect him or her from an emotionally needy spouse.

"Shoshanah," my husband interjected, "I didn't offer them any information. They noticed on their own that you were not your usual outgoing self. Even with all your efforts to cover up, you're pale, weak, and edgy. People pick up on that. Your parents did, too," he added defensively, shifting the blame away from his parents and on to my side of the family.

That night, I quietly sobbed like never before. I felt that I had lost favor with my in-laws. Even though what my husband had told them was only the proverbial tip of the iceberg of what I was truly experiencing, and they did not suspect the true PPD that I in fact had, I felt that I had let my in-laws down. Their catch of an on-the-ball, and happy daughter-in-law was now slightly tainted in their eyes. I felt that I had committed a grave injustice to them, and to my own parents, as well.

Yet at the same time, other thoughts and feelings raged inside me. *Mommy, Daddy!* I silently screamed to my parents. *Imma and Abba!* I wordlessly begged my in-laws. *Help me! Please help us! You are only picking up on a tiny shred of the terrible suffering that I am experiencing. Don't you realize that I am putting on the best act possible in order to save you from anguish—the anguish of watching your daughter and daughter-in-law disintegrate before your eyes into an empty shell?*

It is much worse than what you think. I want to die. I just want to die. I don't want to live with these wrenching emotions and terrifying symptoms. Please help me! **Tell me that you accept me unconditionally** *the way I am;*

*that even if I stay like this for the rest of my life, G-d forbid, you will still always love me and accept me. Please **force** me to get professional help and show me that it is an act of courage to do so—and not an act of weakness. Please teach me, through your own examples, that it does not matter what the rest of the world thinks about emotional and mental illness; that the steps that need to be taken, should be taken, despite society's opinion.*

Mommy and Daddy! Imma and Abba! I continued to cry out silently from my broken and confused heart. *You must help me! I may be a 'big' twenty-four-year-old, but right now I feel scared and as defenseless as this innocent little baby whom I cradle in my arms. You were always the strong, supportive ones, guiding us through life until this point. But despite what I tell you and try to convince you, we need you now more than ever. Please notice my cry for help. It may be silent, but if you listen closely enough, you will hear it; and it's speaking straight to you."*

Chapter Five

My maternity leave was nearing its completion. I needed to pull myself together and go back to work—my job as a speech therapist in a nearby elementary school. As the day of my return drew closer, I vacillated between curling up in a ball on my bed in an anxious stupor, dreading the thought of going back to my job, and actually looking forward to distracting myself from my symptoms by getting back into a steady routine.

As it was, the invasive thoughts and emotions continued to permeate my being at every waking moment during the day. They also continued to disrupt my sleep at night, taking the form of strange and frightening nightmares from which I'd awake in a cold sweat. Whenever my anxiety threatened to overwhelm me, I had to physically clamp my mouth shut so that I shouldn't slip and let on to Baruch about how awful I was feeling. I didn't want him to think that we'd made the wrong decision in ignoring Dr. Roth's advice, so I valiantly continued trying to will away the horrible symptoms by myself.

I tried to prepare a bit. I gathered current reports about the girls in my speech program and attempted to read up a little on the new student being referred to me. I had worked hard to get my speech degree, and I prided myself on working with a professional attitude. I was a popular therapist and took my job very seriously, always on the lookout for new, creative activities that I could do with "my" girls and consistently trying to help them to reach their maximum potential.

Now, however, after many valiant attempts to throw myself back into the "professional speech therapist mode", I realized, to my great consternation and chagrin, that I just could not do so. So much had changed since the last day I had worked at my job before giving birth. Although it was only a couple of months later now, for all intents and purposes, the last time I had worked as a speech therapist with my trademark diligence and creativity could have been a lifetime ago. No matter how much I tried, I simply could not concentrate on my preparation. My usual creative juices had run dry. I had once been able to produce many a novel idea in just a few minutes of effort. Now, though, as I sat, pen in hand and notebook in front of me, trying to brainstorm and think of new ideas and activities, I found my thoughts leading straight to my terrible situation instead.

Again, I began to obsess and worry about the strange thoughts that had clouded my mind for the past weeks. *Do I have a misdiagnosed case of some severe mental illness?* I fretted. *Maybe I've been delusional all these years, and everyone around me has just been humoring me so I just never realized it... And when will I die? What is death, anyway? What really happens after we die? I'm afraid to die, but I feel like dying with all this heaviness on my heart... How long will it take until Baruch's parents convince him to leave me? I hope his new wife will take care of my children— I do love them, after all... Wait! If I love them so much, how could G-d do this to me? I don't understand the ways of G-d, and that bothers me. I want to understand! And while we're on the topic, I don't understand a lot. How could all those innocent people have been murdered in the Holocaust without G-d intervening and saving them, and how could He have let the bus bombings happen in Israel? What happened to all our prayers? Is there really a purpose to them, after all? Wait a minute; a graduate from one of the finest religious schools should know by now that we don't always understand G-d's ways, but that there's always a Master Plan! Where is my trust and faith? What an ingrate I am! No wonder I feel like a wooden block when picking up a prayer book! I bet that I am spiritually flawed because I've unknowingly committed some sin...*

And so it went, my usually rational and logical mind spinning out of control in many directions at once. The most common theme running through my mind was that I was spiritually flawed, and I became paranoid that somehow this was my fault. I also developed a great fear of death and of insanity, and I would ponder both relentlessly. And, of course, I spent a great deal of my time obsessing if, when, and how Baruch would take our kids and abandon me, leaving me to fend for myself in this cold and heartless world.

The night before my scheduled return to work, I could not fall asleep. Tylenol P.M. did not help, and neither did a dose of Benadryl. My body was so wired-up with tension that I simply could not relax enough to drift off, although I was absolutely exhausted. For so long I had been just schlepping through the days and nights, trying to take care of the kids while keeping on my brave front for Baruch, lest he even think of suggesting that I see the doctor whom Dr. Roth had recommended.

The very thought of that happening sent waves of fresh adrenaline through me, jolting me out of my melancholy reverie and willing me to "keep it together" so that I would not have to join the camp of the "mentally ill". The moment I reached out for help, I thought, was the moment I'd be crossing over to "that" side, from which there would be no return. No thought scared me more than that, even with all the countless obsessive and scary notions intruding on my psyche and flooding my mind twenty-four hours a day. The fear of "going crazy" was tantamount to the fear of losing oneself and one's very own identity. What could possibly be more frightening than that?

I will never forget that long, dark, silent night, which I spent alternating between trying to fall asleep in bed and getting up to pace around the apartment. I recall staring out the window at the slumbering city and wondering what the morning would bring. I felt a grave, pervasive sense of danger and all my instincts commanded me to run. *Run? Where should I run to? How could I escape?*

I looked at the murky landscape below our second-floor window and imagined myself running; running with my clothing billowing in the brisk air and my breath coming in jagged gasps; running with a pounding heart and clenched hands; running, running, running, away from it all, until I'd reach the very end of the earth. Perhaps there my sought-after salvation would finally be found…

At seven o'clock the next morning, I pulled myself out of bed and hastily threw on my clothing. I had set out this outfit the previous night with great care, as I was determined to look as "together" as possible in order to present the façade of a calm composure—the complete opposite of how I really felt.

My babysitter was coming over to our apartment to watch Avrami and Devorah, who were still sound asleep. She had been babysitting for Avrami since he was an infant; I liked her and felt comfortable with her. I had no doubt that she would be fine watching two kids. At 8:00 promptly, Estelle rang the bell and marched in.

"Shana, congratulations!" she enthused in her thick Russian accent, enveloping me in a big, heavily perfumed hug. "Now you go work again?"

I smiled bravely and answered in the affirmative.

"Don't worry, Shana, I watch children good. I like children—you know!" Her slightly wrinkled face beamed with pride.

Devorah began to awake in her pink bassinet, whimpering fretfully. Estelle immediately rushed over to her. "Ooh, the new baby! So sweet!" she gushed. She began bustling around, warming up the bottle of formula that I had prepared for the baby.

I felt at ease with Estelle and trusted her expertise. Yet, it was still with great hardship that I kissed a sleeping Avrami and by now howling Devorah goodbye and exited the apartment.

What are you doing? I chided myself. *Leaving your little babies with a virtual stranger! They need their mother!* The fact that everyone around me seemed to be working moms doing the same did not assuage my guilty feelings and heavy heart.

Chapter Five ❖ *61*

My footsteps echoed on the concrete pavement as I headed shakily towards my car. I gingerly stepped inside and sank into the driver's seat. A red light went on in my brain as I realized the danger of driving for the next thirty minutes on virtually no sleep. I'm usually very conscious about safety matters and not a risk-taker by nature. Yet here I was, about to act in an irresponsible and downright dangerous manner. But I felt as if I had no choice. As awful as I was feeling, I just *had* to function like everyone else, or I would be admitting my weakness to all and casting that awful pall of "incompetent" and "unstable" over my solid reputation. So strong was my desire to fit in and be "like everyone else" that I was willing to drive in my exhausted state and risk my very own life, subconsciously internalizing the horrible thought that it was a life not worth very much right now.

Somehow, in G-d's great mercy, I made it safely to school, and soon found myself standing by the door of the school office where all the speech therapists, occupational therapists, and resource teachers were based. I took a deep breath and gripped the metal doorknob with shaky resolve. I then stepped forward and turned the knob slowly, not really knowing what to expect on the other side.

"Shoshanah! Congratulations!" "*Mazel tov*, Shoshanah!" "Congratulations!" "How are you doing?" "What's the baby's name?" Excited and happy voices clamored around me as soon as I entered the small office. I felt the room spinning as I tried to ground myself into reality.

Just smile! I told myself urgently. *Just smile and go along with the show*! And so, with an enormous amount of effort, I pasted on my face the biggest and brightest smile that I could muster.

My colleague and friend, Rivka, came over and hugged me. "Hey, Shoshanah, you lost all your baby weight already! You lucky duck!" She sounded wistful. "That never happens to me," she said.

I just shrugged nonchalantly and continued grinning woodenly. *Dear Rivka, if only you knew why I look so thin!* I thought darkly. *If only you knew that I have trouble swallowing even a spoonful of applesauce or a sip of water, then I doubt you would be feeling any jealousy at all toward me!*

"Hey, you look really tired," commented Hadassah, the director of the preschool division. "Bet your baby is not letting you get any rest!" she said sympathetically, rubbing my shoulder.

"Sort of," I said quietly, sitting down gingerly in a black folding chair that someone had offered me.

Mrs. Hartman, the staff supervisor, soon came in with a couple of early morning announcements pertaining to that day. I tried to listen, but the words just wouldn't penetrate into my fuzzy brain. In fact, they didn't sound like words at all. Instead, they seemed to sound like the crescendo of an erupting volcano or the warning rumbles of an upcoming earthquake. The sense of danger I felt around me was almost palpable.

Snap out of it! I ordered myself harshly. I thought I saw Ayalah, an O.T., peering quizzically at my anxious expression, which made me strengthen my resolve even more. *The last thing you need now, on top of all your other problems, is to let everyone know that you are falling apart!* So I re-pasted the fake smile back on my face and nodded at Mrs. Hartman's words, as if I understood perfectly what she was saying.

All throughout my charade, I tried to force down a lump in my throat that threatened to erupt into full-blown sobs. I also tried to blink away the annoying pricks at the corner of my eyes that threatened to gush into streams of tears.

Why? Just why? I questioned myself over and over. *Why are you about to cry like a 2-year-old child? Did anyone hurt you? Insult you?* I continued berating myself rhetorically. *You have a beautiful new baby, and a secure job with friendly colleagues who wish you well on this milestone in your life. Why on earth do you feel like crying?*

But the answer to this question eluded me, along with the countless other questions I had asked myself in the previous weeks.

I got through that morning by the skin of my teeth. Each girl or group of girls with whom I worked was subject to a spacey speech therapist who gave them old speech exercises to do, and activities that they had already mastered earlier. I just could not concentrate on doing anything novel or creative. As I had already discovered from my feeble attempt at preparation, my brain was in a fog, and all of my inherent creativity was trapped inside, with no way to exit.

Between groups of girls, I shut the door to my little speech room and put my head down on my desk. Each time, my eyes closed on their own accord, as I had been awake for more than twenty-four hours straight at this point. As I'd drift off, disjointed thoughts and images would suddenly come to my mind, all dangerous and threatening. Wildfires, babies screaming, myself falling from high above… I'd shake myself awake every time, utterly convinced that I was on my way to losing my sanity.

Right before I left for the day, I walked to the office to gather my belongings. I was alone for a moment, as I only worked part-time, while the other therapists and resource teachers worked full-time and were thus still occupied with their students. I suddenly felt too drained to move and slumped down in a nearby chair. Gazing off into the distance, I did not notice Mrs. Hartman enter the room and head towards the phone.

"Oh, hello, Shoshanah" she said pleasantly, causing me to jump in surprise. "How was your first day back?"

"Very good," I lied in response, stretching my lips into a smile.

"You look so very tired, Shoshanah," she continued. "Are you getting any sleep?"

"Not really," I answered truthfully with a strained grin. Mrs. Hartman continued to gaze at me carefully, her sharp eyes looking me over. "Shoshanah," she said in a slightly hesitant manner, "are you all right? You seem kind of pensive."

I guess my act did not fool everyone, I thought to myself resignedly. I looked at Mrs. Hartman's open face and warm eyes. I was so tempted to tell her what was going on. I felt like dynamite ready to explode. My feelings and emotions that I was trying so valiantly to suppress kept on pushing their way back again to the surface of my shattered heart. Could I trust Mrs. Hartman? Could I confide in her and ask for some desperately needed advice about how to get out of this treacherous quicksand? Should I tell her about my visit to Dr. Roth? Mrs. Hartman was a wise woman and a mother and grandmother to many; she must have heard of postpartum depression… And here she was, opening the line of communication so naturally for me! I felt like a parched desert traveler being offered a flask of fresh cool water. I needed an objective person in whom to confide, and it seemed that Mrs. Hartman was offering me just that!

As Mrs. Hartman continued to look at me, her kind and intense eyes fixed on my tired ones, waiting for my reply, I began to stammer a response. "I'm-I'm j-just tired; that's all. I'll be fine—honestly!" Before my very own desperate eyes, the flask of water was being slowly poured out, by an old-time archenemy of mine – notoriously known by the name of Pride.

As I headed home a little while later, thinking about my plight and what I had given up just now, my eyes finally released the tears that I had held in check the whole morning. They flowed down my flushed face in hot torrents and blurred my vision. I gripped the steering wheel tightly and pulled over to the side of the road, as I simply couldn't see anything through my tears.

"G-d, You've got to help me!" I sobbed out loud in the privacy of my car. "I can't go on like this much longer. I can't function without sleep anymore. Please, for the sake of the family that You've blessed me with, please help me to cope and be my energetic and capable self again. Please, G-d," I implored, "I'll try to work on myself and improve my character and behavior—whatever You want from me! All I ask of You is for the chance to wake up in the morning feeling refreshed and ready to sing the morning prayer of *Modeh Ani* with my children and serve them breakfast with a smile on my face; a chance to bake cookies with them and push them on the park swings. Please don't deprive me of these simple treasures; now I truly understand that they are the greatest treasures to be found. Please help me, please help me!"

I sat there for a while until my tears were spent. Feeling a sense of catharsis, I relaxed slightly and pondered my options. I soon came to a bold decision. I may not have been brave enough to pour out my heart to Mrs. Hartman, but now I knew that I needed guidance. What did G-d want from me anyhow? I was so utterly confused. I needed to speak to someone whose word I would view as law. And so it was with a sense of determination that I decided to make an appointment to speak with a *rav*, a spiritual mentor. Maybe a *rav* would be able to shed some light on what was happening, and what a Torah-oriented response should be in such a situation. As I came to this conclusion, blessed relief washed through me. I wiped my sopping face and turned the key in the car's ignition. Hoping that the solution to my plight was finally close at hand, I headed home with a sense of serenity that I had not felt in a long time.

Chapter Six

A few days later, I sat across from Rabbi Feld, my husband's dean and mentor, in his small, book-lined study. A variety of scholarly books lay scattered across the *rav's* wide desk. Baruch had vaguely briefed Rabbi Feld of our situation and the reason why I had requested an appointment with him. And so, here I was, carrying sweet little Devorah in her infant seat and facing the well-known community leader. His sharp black eyes pierced through me, but his voice was kind as he asked me, "How can I help you, Mrs. Kagan?"

I put the infant seat down on the wooden floor and began to rock it nervously, although Devorah was already sleeping peacefully in it. The click-clack sound it made seemed to help me relax and collect my racing thoughts.

"Um, Rabbi Feld, I need to speak to you about a private matter," I said in a whisper. I suddenly felt so immature and silly bothering Baruch's Rabbi with my nonsense. But Rabbi Feld looked at me with concerned eyes, encouraging me to continue.

"I just had a baby about two months ago," I continued haltingly, gesturing towards Devorah. "She's a good baby and I'm very grateful for her, but-but I want to know why G-d is punishing me!" The last few words seemed to burst out on their own, and I was shocked at the sudden intensity in my voice.

"Why would you think that G-d is punishing you?" Rabbi Feld asked me calmly.

"Because I'm feeling so horrible, and all I wanted was to build a warm, Jewish home, and obviously I'm not deserving of doing that, because of the terrible thoughts that I have, so I must be inferior to everyone else, because all the other mothers seem to be doing fine, and-and I don't really know why," I ended my rapid torrent of words and stopped to catch my breath.

There was silence in the small room. I stared at the floor in shame, my ever-present tears beginning to emerge again and drop down my flaming cheeks. "Mrs. Kagan," Rabbi Feld began. "Do you think that you are the first woman coming to speak to me after the birth of a baby? The way that you are feeling now and your confused thoughts are quite common after childbirth. Women suffer in different ways during pregnancy and childbirth. For some, it's extreme tiredness and nausea; for some it is high blood pressure; for some it's an excruciating delivery; and for some it's traumatic postpartum symptoms such as the ones that your husband described to me over the phone. It is by no means a punishment, Mrs. Kagan."

"But Rabbi Feld," I said, looking up sharply. "I don't know if you realize what kind of thoughts are floating around in my head. I don't think that other religious people have such thoughts and feelings –but I can't seem to control them!" I quickly added the last line in defense of myself.

"Why don't you tell me about some of these thoughts," Rabbi Feld suggested.

Tell Rabbi Feld some of my thoughts?! I thought to myself, suddenly feeling nauseous. How on earth could I tell Rabbi Feld, head of a renowned yeshivah in a large Jewish community, my heretic thoughts which intruded on my psyche and tormented me?!

My pondering of G-d's ways had evolved into doubts about all that pertained to Judaism In a frantic effort to "cancel out" and negate the thoughts, I would spend hours trying to rationalize them in my head. *Of course the Torah is Divine, because... And evolution has to be a farce, because... The Messiah will definitely be coming at the end, because...* At times, when I'd remain stumped for a proof, I would put down my crying baby who needed to be fed, and run to the bookshelf, frantically skimming through a book on Jewish ideology until I'd find a sentence that would challenge my harassing thought and calm my fears, if only for the moment.

I had concluded that I must be a very intellectual person, with a passion to search for the truth. I tried to congratulate myself on my ever-active mind that needed to be satisfied with deep intellectual pursuits. But something didn't fit with that line of reasoning. While I had always been blessed with an inquisitive mind and solid intelligence, I had never been the type to engage my teachers in fiery debates about esoteric topics. In fact, I had always found those high school discussions somewhat pointless, as they never seemed to get anywhere. I was a practical person who liked to apply knowledge to real life and everyday situations. As for the heavy-duty theological questions and ponderings of the origin of G-d? Back in school, I had filed them away on the back burner. It was enough for me to see the beauty and symmetry of our intricate world to recognize instinctively that there was a Creator. And by seeing how He provided for all of His creations, I felt assured that I would be taken care of, too. Of course I had wondered about tough topics such as reward and punishment, death, the afterlife—like every thinking human being does—but these kinds of questions had never gnawed at my brain the way they were doing so now. I had understood intellectually that if 99% of what I saw made sense and had an explainable reason, which we learned about through our studies, then that remaining 1% must have a Divine plan behind it, too. This awareness of G-d's Master Plan on a cosmic level made me content to leave things running in His hands. But now I found that doubt had entered my psyche, jeeringly demanding solid and irrefutable answers for that 1% of the questions whose answers humans simply cannot comprehend—and it was demanding those answers *now!*

I know now that what was happening was that I was suffering from a form of Obsessive Compulsive Disorder, which can manifest itself after childbirth as a component of PPD. This disorder focuses on the doubts that all human beings must live with, and causes sufferers to spend an endless amount of time trying to negate the troubling thoughts and feelings that the doubts bring on. I was engaging in a form of mental ritualizing whereby I felt compelled to try and quiet my obsessive thoughts by finding "proofs" to counteract them. I was, in essence, trying to reach a level of certainty that no human being can ever have, as G-d chose to leave room for doubt in the world, so that we could have *bechirah*—free choice.

No amount of intellectual "proofs" could ever quiet my racing thoughts, because these thoughts were not coming from an intellectual source, as I had erroneously surmised. The thoughts were the products of a real illness, and could not be cured by my going to lectures and reading philosophy books. In fact, when I attempted to quiet the thoughts by doing so, I was actually feeding the illness even more!

Of course, at the time, I did not know too much about OCD. All I'd heard about it were some vague details, such as it being a strange illness where people washed their hands a lot. Since I didn't have that symptom, it never occurred to me that what I had was a form of OCD. All I knew was that I felt tremendous guilt, like I was the lowest of the low. After all, I was religious from birth, had been given an extensive Jewish education, and was well-read in Jewish literature. Why was I having all these doubts? I had no excuse in the world to have them! As such, I was horrified by Rabbi Feld's suggestion that I share some of my thoughts with him.

How could I tell him that when I prayed, these heretic thoughts would spring up with such force and vigor that it pained me to open a prayer book? How could I tell him about the countless philosophical questions, questions that I never knew I had, which had suddenly appeared and persisted on hammering away at my exhausted brain, with no respite? And what about the innate feeling of holiness that I had always experienced while lighting the the Sabbath candles and saying the holy Jewish prayer of Shema Yisrael? How could I explain to Rabbi Feld that this beautiful feeling had disappeared from my life, leaving me feeling cold, empty, and devoid of all spirituality and meaning in my existence?

I couldn't possibly tell him all of this! But Rabbi Feld was looking at me expectantly, so I tried to give him a vague answer. "Just thoughts that bother me during prayer and make me feel kind of numb," I mumbled.

Rabbi Feld's sharp yet empathetic eyes seemed to bore into me as I gave him this feeble answer. "Let me tell you about thoughts, Mrs. Kagan," he said, his voice firm and clear. "A thought is just that—a thought. A nebulous, intangible concept. We all have thoughts that are unwanted, especially when we are in emotional distress. G-d does not expect us to never have unwanted thoughts in our heads. What He does expect of us is that we not act negatively as a result of them. In other words, although our *reaction* to our thoughts *is* in our control, the thoughts themselves *are not*.

"In fact," Rabbi Feld continued, "we all have thoughts that we usually keep in check subconsciously. Our minds paste big red 'stop signs' on these thoughts and don't allow them to emerge into our consciousness. But at stressful times, such as after childbirth for a woman, these 'stop signs' are sometimes ripped off and the thoughts emerge and begin bothering the person. But Mrs. Kagan, there is no danger involved here. Like I said, there is nothing wrong with a person having such thoughts in his head. It is not a reflection on one's character or spiritual status. In fact, it is usually those who are spiritually sensitive who are so distressed at such thoughts! So," he chuckled lightly, "feel free to think these thoughts on purpose as much as you need to! This will help you to see these thoughts for what they are—nothing but silly little thoughts—and your fear of them will be dispelled. Go ahead; think these thoughts! You have my permission!" he said with a grin.

I was shocked at his words. *Think these thoughts intentionally?!* It was the exact opposite approach as what I had been doing! I'd been trying so hard to push the thoughts *out of my mind*, although they continued to follow me relentlessly. Even now, as I sat and spoke to Rabbi Feld, I was simultaneously trying to ward off the "evil" thoughts.

Having Rabbi Feld's "permission" to think my awful thoughts initially lifted a tremendous load off my shoulders. *Maybe I'm not that terrible, heretical person that I thought I was, after all!* I thought to myself. But my feelings of relief were tempered with uncertainty, as my ever-present doubt, which couldn't stand when I felt reassured, immediately jumped in with its own argument: *What if he does not understand my problem properly and is guiding me wrongly?* It was just too much to shift my anxious perspective in such a rapid manner.

Still, though, I suddenly felt that I had the courage to continue speaking with the *rav*. "Rabbi Feld," I said slowly, "what exactly does G-d want from me? Here He gave me these precious children, and I'm all prepared to raise them according to His will. But I'm stuck—stuck in place, unable to bring forth the creativity and enthusiasm that lie within me, the tools that I need to run a healthy household and raise my children. I feel as if I am being served a gourmet dinner, but my mouth is taped shut. I'm so frustrated and confused!"

Rabbi Feld listened attentively to my impassioned words and then leaned forward to answer me. "Mrs. Kagan, the first thing that I would like to tell you before we discuss anything deeper is a very practical piece of advice. It would be quite beneficial for you and your family if you would enlist plenty of household help—whatever you need to help things run smoothly during this difficult period, so that you won't feel so overwhelmed. If you can't afford it, there are volunteer organizations that can help out. You must realize that there is no requirement to be a martyr and push yourself to your limits, especially at such a time."

"But I'm very capable of household work!" I forcefully interjected. "Why should I let someone take over what is my duty?"

"No, Mrs. Kagan," Rabbi Feld said, looking me straight in the eye. "Your obligation now is to take care of yourself, so that in turn, you will be able to take care of your family. That is your job now. Yes, it would be an obligation for you to... go by yourself to a mall and go window shopping! Or to go to the library and read Huckleberry Finn! If you do these light, leisurely activities in order to recoup your physical and emotional health, then in the whole scheme of things, your household will thrive."

I mulled over Rabbi Feld's surprising words as he continued to speak. "As for why this Divine test is being inflicted upon you, that is something that neither I nor anyone else can answer. We must recognize that nothing is by chance, and even if we don't know the reason why some things happen, we have faith that G-d is good and that the hardships He sends us are actually for our benefit." Noting my strained expression and hunched shoulders, he added sympathetically, "Though it is hard to always internalize this fact."

Yes, it certainly is hard to internalize this fact! I thought to myself. Even as I trusted Rabbi Feld and intuitively knew that he was speaking words of truth, it was so difficult to comprehend what good could possibly come out of this quagmire in which I found myself. In fact, I couldn't believe for a moment that I would ever feel well again. The thick cloud of despair which I found myself in left no room for any ray of light to penetrate. Although I heard and intellectually understood Rabbi Feld's words, emotionally, I just couldn't accept them.

"What if I don't pass this test?" I asked hesitantly. "What if I just snap and lose it, G-d forbid? I don't want this test if there is a chance I might fail!" I said in a fearful whisper. My heartbeat was already starting to accelerate at the mere thought.

Rabbi Feld smiled. "Guess what, Mrs. Kagan?" he said. "You are stronger than you think! There are many days when people fear that they might lose themselves in their legitimate problems, but they have no choice but to go on with life until, eventually, they are over the hump—and they see that they've survived! Our Creator infused us all with enormous reservoirs of untapped emotional fortitude. One day, you'll look back at this period in your life and you'll be surprised at how you weathered this storm. In fact, you'll see that there was even some good that came out of it."

"You mean one day I really might 'look back' at this rough time? Do you really believe that I will eventually feel like myself again? That these horrible symptoms will pass?" I asked, a glimmer of hope in my voice.

"Yes, I do believe that all of this will pass for you," Rabbi Feld replied. "Just as it has passed for the many other new mothers whom I have counseled."

"It's hard to believe that others go through the same anguish. All of my peers seem to be just fine," I muttered to myself as Rabbi Feld stood up and began walking me to the door.

He overheard my comment and gave me a warm smile. "You know what? You seem relatively all right from the outside, as well. No one can ever truly know what is going on inside of his neighbor's heart."

Standing at the door and about to turn the doorknob, I suddenly stopped. "Rabbi Feld," I said, grasping Devorah's infant seat tightly with both of my hands, "there is one more point that I feel very unsure about. It's-it's about taking medication." I felt my cheeks get warm, and my voiced dropped to a whisper. "Should I, or shouldn't I?"

"I'm sorry, Mrs. Kagan," Rabbi Feld said gently, "but I am not able to answer that question. You need to speak to a qualified doctor and get his opinion about that."

"Okay," I said resignedly. I had so hoped that Rabbi Feld would direct me in this area for, although I had made up my mind not to take medication, deep down I knew that my decision was based solely on my pride.

"Thank you, Rabbi Feld," I said shyly. "I appreciate your time and advice."

"It was my pleasure, Mrs. Kagan," Rabbi Feld said warmly. "You'll see—everything will have been worth it in the end," he added as he patted Devorah's pink cheek. "And may you and your husband merit to build a beautiful home with blessing, success and health!"

"Amen," I answered with all my heart, silently imploring G-d to fulfill Rabbi Feld's blessing, and soon. "Amen."

Chapter Seven

If I'd expected my talk with Rabbi Feld to bring me instant relief, I was sorely disappointed. Although I was comforted by the *rav's* words, and truly felt reassured that I wasn't a bad person and that I wasn't being punished in any way, I continued to suffer from agonizing symptoms that darkened my days and lengthened my nights. In this way, the days and weeks passed by. I still stubbornly refused to get psychological help—although at this point, Baruch was pleading with me to do it. But I felt that I just couldn't face that option, because, to my mind, doing so would be tantamount to obtaining a stamp of failure for myself. I also couldn't shake the thought that if I would be seen at a psychologist or psychiatrist's office, our family's social lives would be ruined, and our children's future would be adversely affected.

If I go for psychological help, the torment of shame would be too great to bear, I tried to convince myself, *and that would break me completely; I just know it. Instead, I'm going to grit my teeth and stick this out for as long as I can.*

This is what I'd stoically tell myself during my "up" moments. But in the pitch black of the long night, when I'd be tossing and turning in the throes of a choking panic attack, I would highly doubt my decision. I'd be tempted to make an appointment with a mental health professional the very next morning. However, when morning would arrive and I would painstakingly pull myself out of bed to attend to the children, bleary-eyed and dizzy, my ego would invariably resurface and remind me of my pledge to remain "normal". Going for professional help would be crossing a certain boundary, the boundary that separated those who were "normal" from those who were not. And I was not about to cross that boundary and receive the title "abnormal" or "crazy" just yet.

I kept up my façade for a few months, suffering in silence. Then one day, to my utter shock and dismay, I found out that I was pregnant! At this point in my life, pregnancy was not something I was expecting to happen. I had vaguely explained my precarious situation to my doctor, and had asked for an appropriate form of birth control to use for the foreseeable future. Apparently, however, I had not explained well enough just how precarious my state truly was, because the birth control my doctor had prescribed for me was obviously not the most effective one.

I felt extremely angry and betrayed when I found out about my new pregnancy. Here I was, barely hanging on to my own life, and now I was supposed to bring a new life into the world while I was still experiencing my horrible symptoms?! I was angry at my doctor for recommending a form of protection that had not accomplished its intended goal, and for not picking up on the sense of urgency I felt when I'd consulted with him.

Now, looking back at these events, I realize how unfair and impartial I was being. The reason the doctor hadn't understood the gravity of my predicament, and thus did not suggest a more foolproof plan of action, was because, as usual, I'd been trying to save face and downplay how I truly felt. The attitude I'd given over was that I simply needed a few months to "get myself together" and then I'd be ready to reclaim my position as Supermom, all set to achieve the impossible. So what did I expect—that my doctor should read my mind in order to know the *real* issues that I had, the truly dangerous state in which I was?! This incident taught me very well the importance of being completely honest when asking for medical guidance, especially when the question pertains to an area of such personal nature as this.

What was it like to have postpartum depression while being pregnant at the same time? Draining, to say the least. My problem of not being able to fall asleep was finally over, only to be replaced with an equally distressing problem of not being able to stay awake. My body was under tremendous physical stress, trying to recover from a very recent pregnancy while simultaneously maintaining a brand new one.

The physical and emotional strain created within me exhaustion so deep that I was virtually powerless against it. I literally could not keep my eyes open at times and constantly felt as if I was enveloped in a huge, dense fog of lethargy. The children spent countless hours unattended on our little porch as I lay on the nearby couch, too drained to move. The simplest of chores would be neglected for days, as I tried in vain to swim against this powerful current. To top it off, I suffered from horrible morning sickness for about five months and could barely eat, which weakened me even further.

I would wake up in the morning, overcome with nausea and a heavy fatigue. With Baruch's help, I'd get the kids ready for the babysitter. Then I'd drag myself to work, where I'd be met with a chock-full schedule of students awaiting my speech intervention. When I look back at this time, I am absolutely amazed that I was able to continue working even in such a weak state. I think that I instinctively knew that my work was my emotional lifeline during this traumatic time, as it proved to distract me somewhat from my overwhelming, dark thoughts and powerful feelings, so I threw myself into it regardless of how I felt.

Still, though, I recall feeling at times so sick and exhausted, that I would often put my students on the school's computers and let them play educational games while I catnapped in the corner. As far as the nights went—I honestly don't even remember them. Exhausted, I would fall asleep together with the children at about 7:00 p.m. and then proceed to sleep until morning. I literally could not keep my eyes open past my kids' bedtime. In the middle of the night, through my hazy dreams, I would hear little Devorah crying and Baruch puttering in the nearby kitchen, preparing a warm bottle for her. I think that Baruch, who normally needs a great deal of quality sleep, was given an extra gift of strength from Above in order to help keep our family together; otherwise, he would have surely collapsed under the tension and strain.

I remember feeling oh-so-artificial and fake when responding to people's surprised yet joyful comments, once I put back on my maternity clothing and my pregnancy became apparent to all. I'd dutifully turn up my lips at the appropriate times, though inside I'd be seething at the unfairness of it all. Of course I would love to bring another precious soul into this world and into our family—but not right now! I felt like I was just beginning to get my life back together after Devorah's birth. For the first time since my symptoms had started, I'd recently begun to feel the slightest trace of firm ground beneath my shaky legs, and now suddenly—boom! The ground had violently opened up again, with no prior warning! How was I supposed to be a good mother to this innocent new life that was fluttering around within me? I already held a bitter grudge against the poor soul, as if it were taunting me as it got ready for its arrival here on this world. Dejectedly, I wondered if I'd ever be able to manage after the birth. What would happen to my poor children?

But lo and behold, when our baby boy Moshe Dovid was born, I was okay! It was almost as if his birth had miraculously re-shuttled my pregnancy-related hormones back into a more controlled setting after the roller coaster ride of Devorah's birth. I was certainly not all bright and cheery, but I felt like a typical, tired and overwhelmed new mother. I had my moments when I experienced familiar frightening symptoms, but nothing to the degree of intensity and misery that I'd felt the year before. And my secret fear that I wouldn't be able to love and care for my baby? Thankfully, it was for naught. I grew to love little Moshe Dovid as fiercely as my other children, and in a very short time I recognized what blessing this sweet little boy brought to our home.

As a result of having three children so close in age, I was encouraged by my family to cut down my work to only three days a week. I was given a lot of encouragement and admiration on how well I was raising the kids. People somehow excused the by-now constant mess in our formerly neat and orderly home, and smiled at the sight of all three of our cute kids squeezed together in our well-used twin carriage, with me pushing them from behind. I reveled in these figurative pats on the back, and felt that with Divine assistance, I had achieved the impossible. This had a positive effect on my ego and postpartum recovery.

Slowly but surely, I began to feel more and more like my old self. By the time Moshe Dovid was about a year old, I was completely fine. It was like the past twenty-two months of upheaval were over and done with. Like a deep and dark fog dissipating after a fast and furious storm, the heavy memories receded and finally faded away into oblivion.

I was my happy and energetic self again, exulting in my daily whirlwind of taking care of three active toddlers. I never let myself dwell on those terrifying months when I had been so "out of it". In fact, I never let myself read about any psychological ailment in health periodicals or in books, because I was scared that it would stir up those awful memories. I was "over and done with" those horrible days, and I never wanted to go back to that deep, dark abyss of despair again. Keeping far, far away from anything that had to do with that terrifying time period was my childish way of protecting myself.

I was proud that I had been brave enough to weather the storm myself, and congratulated myself on my emotional fortitude. *You see? You were absolutely right! You did not need to see any psychiatrist whatsoever, like Dr. Roth recommended! Thank G-d, you pulled through all by yourself!*

Oh, how wonderful it was to be me again! The fact that I had recovered naturally after Moshe Dovid's birth, like most other mothers, was my "proof" that I was cured forever. I felt that I had earned the right to be just a tiny bit smug, and I continually told myself, *obviously, strong people like you can ward off any illness!*

Yet, in the deep recesses of my heart and mind, nagging thoughts and feelings questioned my authoritative stance regarding my mental health. Even as I promised myself again and again that the emotional illness which I had fought against for so many months was now over for good, I was still haunted by three ominous words, words that were embedded so deeply into my subconscious, that during my action-packed day I was barely even aware of them. Nevertheless, at times, no matter how doggedly I'd brush them aside, they would defiantly pop back into my mind. Those words, seemingly small and insignificant, yet laden with meaning, were: Will it return?

Chapter Eight

"Congratulations! You have a beautiful baby boy!" exclaimed my obstetrician, Dr. Gupta. I lay back against my pillow and whispered my thanks to the One Above. Another healthy child, Thank G-d! How blessed I was!

I smiled at Baruch across the room, my intense ecstasy mirrored in his joyful eyes. "*Mazel tov*, Shoshanah!" he said in a voice filled with emotion. "And welcome to the world, little prince!" he murmured to our wriggling pink-faced son who was bellowing loudly in Patricia, the labor and delivery nurse's, hands as she attempted to measure and weigh him.

"Wow, you've got a whopper of a son!" Patricia commented as she took him off the scale. "Nine pounds, eight ounces, and twenty-two inches long! He must take after Daddy, huh?" She gave a chuckle, glancing at Baruch's six-foot-one-inch frame.

"I guess so!" Baruch laughingly replied as he watched the nurse swaddle our newborn in a tiny, soft blanket.

Finally, the moment I was waiting for arrived. Patricia handed over the squalling bundle into my outstretched arms. Although this baby was my fourth child to be born, I still felt as if he was my very first. The overwhelming joy and gratitude that I felt at my children's births never diminished in quantity or intensity. I was always left with feelings of wonder and deep awe at the marvelous workings of G-d. I was holding a bundle of potential, a little *soul* whose angelic aura hinted at the majestic spiritual world he had just left behind.

I buried my face into my son's silken features, feeling his rapid little breaths against my flushed cheeks—his very first breaths in this new world in which he found himself.

"So, Shoshanah," Baruch said happily, shifting my attention towards him, "we need a name for this little prince. Which one should we use from the names that we discussed—Aharon, Yaakov, or Daniel?"

"Baruch," I said with sudden longing in my voice, "I want to name him Ezriel."

"Ezriel?" Baruch was clearly taken aback. "That wasn't one of the names that we discussed!"

"I know," I said, "but it's a name that means so much to me and suits this occasion so perfectly." Passion filled my voice as I continued. "Ezriel—which means G-d is my help. Hasn't G-d helped me? Hasn't He brought me to this stage and held my hand throughout? Look at where we are today. Our fourth child has just arrived! When I think back to that horrible period when Devorah was born…" My voice drifted off slightly as my mind flashed back to those devastating days. "You know, Baruch, at that time, I truly thought that I was not capable of having any more children. But here we are today, only five short years later, with our fourth child! I recognize that I received help from Above, and I want to express my appreciation to G-d…" I fell silent, suddenly feeling a wave of exhaustion come over me as the events of the last few hours began to catch up with my body. For the first time, I became aware of the tremendous pain I was in, as the local anesthetic I had received was beginning to wear off.

Baruch noticed my tiredness and quickly went to get the nurse. Patricia entered the room, and I gave her the baby to bring to the nursery. Finally, I was able to close my weary eyes. Baruch took the hint and, murmuring a quick goodbye, left the room to make some very exciting phone calls. Our discussion over our baby's name came to a swift halt for the moment.

Eight days passed, and I found myself standing in the crowded synagogue for Ezriel's circumcision ceremony. Standing close to my family, my hands tightly clutching my prayer book, I listened to my baby being named: "*V'yikarei shemo b'Yisrael—And his name will be called in Israel—Ezriel son of Baruch Tzvi Hersh...*"

I closed my eyes briefly and tried to squeeze my prayers for this little boy all together at this most auspicious moment. I prayed that little Ezriel should grow up to be an asset to his people, that he should be a healthy and happy child, unhindered by misfortune or conflict. As I thought about all my dreams and aspirations that I had for baby Ezriel, whom I'd come to cherish in the last eight days, the tears began to fall. But these were tears of which I was not ashamed, and I thanked G-d from the bottom of my heart for all of His kindnesses.

Then the ceremony was over, and the people around me began to congratulate me and wish me "*mazel tov*". Many of our guests inquired about our babies name. "It was just a beautiful name," I explained repeatedly. *And the rest of the reason is not your business!* I added silently as I kissed the women around me and accepted their good wishes.

Finally, when little Ezzy could wait no longer, I retreated to a side room and fed my precious baby. How I loved him so much! Holding him close, I vowed to take care of the priceless gift that I held in my arms. I smoothed his fuzzy brown hair and allowed him to grip my pinky finger tightly with his tiny hand. I silently offered my promise to take care of him to the best of my ability, come what may. Was it a coincidence, or did I see his little body relax and his lips turn up as a result of my silent pledge?

Days passed and merged into weeks. I was busy running my lively household and was barely aware of time passing. Before I knew it, it was time for my six-week postpartum check-up. I bundled up little Ezzi and off we went for a visit to Dr. Gupta in her office located in Memorial Hospital's maternity unit. Walking down the white tiled floors and passing the labor and delivery unit, I once again felt mesmerized by the awesome kindness of G-d. Here I had walked, a mere six-and-a-half weeks before, trudging ever so slowly and painfully as I tried to keep my balance steady while I signed in for the delivery. And now, here I was, twenty-five pounds lighter, holding a healthy and perfectly formed Ezzy in his navy-blue infant seat. I was buoyed by these cheerful thoughts and walked into the doctor's office in an effusive mood.

"Hi, Mrs. Kagan!" called out the friendly, booming voice of Denise, the receptionist. "How is that baby chick doing?" Grinning widely, she leaned her ample frame over her white desk to take a quick peek at the baby. I smiled, again feeling as though this was my first child, and held Ezzy up to her so she could get a better look at him. I spent the next fifteen minutes answering Denise's questions about Ezzy's temperament and sleeping schedule, until I was called in to the exam room.

I placed Ezzy's infant seat in the corner of the room and sat down on the long, narrow exam table, waiting for Dr. Gupta to arrive. Suddenly, to my surprise, I noticed on the table a small white slip of paper with five prepared questions for me to fill out. Curiously, I scanned the questions and read:

Please rate yourself on the following, using a scale from 0-10.

Do you find yourself crying a lot for no apparent reason?

Do you find that your sleep patterns have changed drastically?

Do you entertain thoughts of harming yourself or your baby?

Have you experienced a significant loss or gain of appetite?

Are you experiencing feelings of panic or extreme apprehension?

Wow! I thought to myself appreciatively. *I wish that they would have had this postpartum depression screening years ago when Devorah was born. I sure would've benefitted from it then!* With a sting, I realized that had I answered truthfully back then, all my answers would have been a resounding "yes," rating very high on the 0-10 scale. But my thoughts quickly flipped to a more positive bend, as I realized with gratitude that this time around, all of my answers were, an emphatic "no". So I joyously filled out the form, placing a 0 next to each question with joy and appreciation in my heart. Thank G-d, I was out of that black hole!

Or was I?

About two weeks later, we had a family celebration—a bar mitzvah—that was being held in a nearby city. I recall feeling inexplicably slightly "off" early that week, a bit short of breath and edgy, although nothing too worrisome. Also, I was absolutely exhausted, as the baby had become increasingly fussy lately and had not been sleeping well. Despite all this, though, it didn't enter our minds to not attend the bar mitzvah, so we packed up our minivan early Friday morning and headed out of town for the event.

Right away, I knew that it was a mistake to have come. The weekend was very stressful. Our accommodations were cramped and unpleasant, as we squeezed together in the dank one-room basement of a family who had offered to put up relatives of the bar mitzvah boy for the weekend. The children, overtired and disoriented in their unfamiliar environment, were unruly and argumentative. I was very overwhelmed, and berated myself for making the trip. Surely my relatives would have understood if I had missed the celebration; after all, Ezzy was just two months old!

We arrived home Sunday afternoon, but it took a while to get the kids back on to some sort of schedule. To top it off, Devorah and Moshe Dovid came down with a nasty stomach virus and were quite ill. I was constantly changing their bed sheets and trying to get them to drink fluids, as they seemed to be on the verge of dehydration. By mid-week, they had finally recovered, yet I still felt depleted by the stress of the last few days.

My feelings of vague unease continued to escalate bit by bit, although things were still mostly normal. But then, a day or two later, boom! Like a sonic rocket, my world crashed, unraveling with the speed and intensity of a ferocious summer storm.

It was Thursday morning and the kids were all finally back at school. It was deliciously quiet in the house and I was enjoying the solitude. I was calmly feeding little Ezzy on my cozy glider, when suddenly, for no reason at all, my heart began to pound violently. A feeling of deep, deep dread gripped me, and the room began to swim before my eyes. I felt sweat forming on my face and watched my hands begin to shake tremulously.

Oh, no. No, no, no, a thousand times no! Not that again! Please, G-d, anything but that...

Sure enough, "it" was back. That encounter was only the beginning, as I once again began having trouble breathing; I lost my appetite completely, and remained awake virtually the entire night, shaking with fear and covered in a cold sweat. Knowing from the past what was happening to me and petrified of what I knew was likely yet to come, I became almost immobilized with fear. The frightening and obsessive thoughts returned with a deep vengeance, as if livid about their forced imprisonment for the last five years.

The realization that I was suffering from PPD again came as a complete shock to me. The fact that I was older, had more experience raising children, and was more secure in my marriage had given me the assurance that this terrible affliction would never come my way again. I had long ago forgotten, for all practical purposes, what those horrible feelings and symptoms felt like. It was a big black spot in my past that I was determined to forget, and I was sure that I never would go there again.

Baruch was also dismayed when he found out that I was not doing well. The memories of those months of hardship, during which he'd taken over the role of mother and father, came rushing back to him. He tried to convince me to not rush to any conclusions before I diagnosed myself with Postpartum Depression. "Maybe you're just a little overwhelmed?" he asked, the poignant hope in his voice making my heart break. But deep within me, I knew the truth: The dreaded illness, from which I had suffered silently for twenty-two months of my life, was back.

Once again, I tried hard to fight it. I tried relaxation tapes, self-help books, and getting extra babysitting help. But my life was so much more complicated now. I had four very active, young children, had just switched from a part-time job to a position which held more responsibility and hours, and my husband, no longer in yeshivah, had a much tighter and more pressured schedule than what he'd had five years ago. In fact, Baruch was barely ever home now. There was no way his job responsibilities would ever allow for him to take over parts of my role, the way he had done so during my previous bout with PPD. I felt doomed from the start, realizing clearly that without intervention, I would not be able to swing it this time. In fact, I realized, if things continued like this, the illness could, G-d forbid, progress even further than it had last time.

One Tuesday morning, as I tried to give the children breakfast, I reached my breaking point. As I held a screaming Ezzy and hazily watched the other three kids, half-dressed, running around wildly, I put my head down on the kitchen table and began to sob. The cereal all over the floor and my messy-looking children, who were intent on misbehaving during my weakest moments, were just too much for me. Young Avrami, Devorah, and Moshe Dovid stopped in their tracks and looked at their weeping mother in bewilderment and fright.

They stood there, seemingly immobilized, watching me with their innocent wide eyes. Even Ezzy quieted down for a moment and gazed at me, a look of wonder on his little face. Then Avrami, my big boy, who was all of eight years old, asked in a frightened voice, "Mommy, why are you crying?" Too choked up to reply, I just continued to cry, trying to muffle the sounds by covering my face with my shaking hands. Ezzy's wails soon joined mine once again, as he waved his tight little fists around in the air. The other children, confused and frightened, quietly left the kitchen, and I was left alone—alone with a crying baby—to ponder my situation.

It suddenly dawned on me that I was I was a fool for thinking that I was out of the woods forever. Here I was, again stuck in the thorny thickets, again with no clear direction of where to go next. All my pride about having such inner strength, about being able to handle my emotions so successfully, and about having cured myself of my PPD last time, without any help or medical intervention, fell flat with one big swoop. Simultaneously, conflicting thoughts whirled around in my aching head and confused feelings simmered in my tortured soul. *Wait!* I thought indignantly. *Haven't I already suffered enough from this sickness? I served my time! And here I even named my son "Ezriel" in an attempt to offer my humble "thank you" to G-d for getting me out of it. I am not an ingrate! I had gratitude; I spoke to a rabbi to get spiritual guidance. Why, oh, why, am I being afflicted again? It just seems so unfair!* My anguished heart demanded answers, but no answer seemed to be coming soon.

Thinking about my distraught children, I knew that I did not have the luxury of waiting for things to pan out by themselves again, or for the magical answer to suddenly "appear". For what if I had to wait too long, or even forever, for that to happen, G-d forbid? What irrevocable damage could be done to my precious family? In the five years that had passed since I had last experienced these heart-wrenching symptoms, I had fortunately matured somewhat, and now my own pride was no longer my sole concern. I was frightened for the safety and stability of my children.

Somehow, I managed to send the older kids off to school, not even caring what their teachers would think about their unkempt appearances. Then I called Baruch on his cell phone, feeling guilty all the while, as I knew that I was disrupting him from his work.

"Baruch," I cried to him, "please help me! I have reached rock bottom. What am I supposed to do?"

Baruch sent the ball back into my court by tentatively asking me, "Shoshanah, what do you want to do?"

Then I said it. "I need professional help," I whispered. "This time I can't do it alone."

Baruch, my wonderful and sensitive husband, reassured me that he would stand by my side, and he encouraged me to take the leap.

I hung up the phone and distractedly began tending to Ezzy. My hands moved, changing his diaper, dressing him, and feeding him, but my thoughts were far away. Was I ready to take the step that I had fought against for so long? Listening to my inner voice, which, in its newfound maturity, was beginning to combine the heart and the mind, I concluded that for the sake of my dear family, and for my sake as well, the answer to that question was a resounding yes.

And so, with great reluctance and enormous fear, I stepped off my proverbial high horse and headed for the phone. I pondered for a moment just whom to call for help. My mind flashed to my OB-GYN, Dr. Gupta. *But she knows you, and as of just a few weeks ago, you just told her how wonderful you're feeling!* My shame and embarrassment kept me from contacting her.

Left with no recourse, I began flipping through the Yellow Pages until I came across a familiar-sounding name, Dr. Carmia, and within moments, I was speaking with her secretary. I had heard Dr. Carmia's name once or twice and vaguely remembered hearing that she was supposed to be a specialist in her field—the field of adult psychiatry.

Chapter Nine

My trembling hands attempted to fill out the mounds of paperwork that lay before me. I was sitting in a soft maroon lounge chair in Dr. Carmia's office. As a new patient, I was required to fill out all of the appropriate forms. I signed my name to hospital consent forms and filled out a number of questionnaires assessing all the scary-sounding symptoms that a patient could have, such as violent thoughts and suicide attempts... My heart dropped a little lower and my discomfort grew with each page. I was frightened out of my wits. Even more terrifying was the possibility of being seen here by someone I knew! I kept checking the doorway, but thankfully, I did not see anyone whom I recognized.

After finishing the paperwork, I concentrated on looking intently at my shoes, the carpet, my clenched fists...anywhere but into the eyes of the few other people who were sitting quietly in the large waiting room. I kept waiting to hear the frantic babbles of some unfortunate patient having a psychotic breakdown, or perhaps the monotone of an alleged psychopath, but all I heard was the rustling of magazine pages being turned and read by the other patients who, to my surprise, seemed like regular people. *I wonder what they're here for*, I thought silently to myself. Suddenly, I became aware of a high-pitched, yapping sound in the room.

I looked up and tried to trace the unusual sound, which sounded like a puppy to me. Suddenly, a very slight and diminutive woman, heavily made up with all sorts of cosmetics and leading a small, furry brown dog on a short black leash, came down the hall and entered the waiting room. Click-clacking around in her very high heels, she called my name in a clipped voice. With a shocking realization, I realized that this lady was none other than Dr. Carmia herself!

For the first time in a long while, I felt a bubble of laughter well up in my stomach. This woman appeared absolutely wacky with her garish make-up and the way she kept crooning to her dog! I hesitantly got up and followed her, keeping my distance from the yapping puppy. She briskly led me to her plant-filled office, explaining to me that she used "Frisky," her dog, to facilitate healing in some of her patients whom she would be seeing later today. That made some sense to me, but the scene still felt quite surreal! I felt like I was in some bizarre and comical high school play in which I was playing a lead role. But my giggles quickly died down when I reminded myself of the reason why I was here, and I realized that this woman, strange-looking though she was, might be the very messenger whom I needed to get me out of my predicament.

As soon as we were seated, Dr. Carmia began. "So, Mrs. Kagan, tell me what brings you here."

Jumping right in at her offer, I quickly related to her all the disabling symptoms that I was experiencing. I told her about my past experience with Postpartum Depression and how the disorder was resurfacing again now, after baby number four. I explained to her the severity of my symptoms and how they were interfering with my life, as well as with my family's. I ended my speech with an urgent plea. "Can you help me?"

Dr. Carmia looked at me seriously. Although she appeared strange and quirky, her voice was professional and pragmatic, yet not at all warm in nature. "Mrs. Kagan, you will feel better. You would be surprised to know just how many other women have similar symptoms after childbirth. Why, just last week, I had a mom come crying that she has obsessive and bizarre thoughts of sticking her newborn into the microwave!" She smiled at me, waiting for me to respond. I did not smile back. Thoughts of that nature were not funny to me when I was going through this. In fact, I was afraid of hearing anything disturbing, as ridiculous as it sounded, for fear that the thought would "stick" to my brain and begin to torment me as well.

"Sounds to me like you would be a good candidate for taking an anti-depressant," Dr. Carmia continued in her clipped voice. "Your daily routine is being quite affected, and you have a past history. I'm going to write you out a prescription for Zoloft." She reached for her prescription pad.

"Okay," I answered numbly. As much as I dreaded taking this step, I accepted the situation. I knew that I couldn't go through another two years of agony now. There was too much at stake; I had too many responsibilities at this point in my life. My husband and children needed me to be happy and healthy, and, I knew, I needed myself to be happy and healthy. Because I, as a human being, had to have my needs met as well as any other person did.

As I sat there and watched Dr. Carmia write out the prescription, I tried hard to make sense of the questions whirling around in my head. Would this strange doctor really be able to help me? Was I supposed to be asking her anything? Did I need psychotherapy as well?

Dr. Carmia asked me to make an appointment for a follow-up visit in six weeks. Then she began gathering my file, obviously ending our meeting. As I got up to leave, I finally found my voice. "How long will it take until I feel better?" I asked her. "And are there any side effects?"

"It will be at least six weeks until the medication builds up enough in your bloodstream to make a difference, so you won't really feel a change until then," she answered crisply. "And as for your other question, this is a very commonly used and safe medication, and it has few side effects." After pronouncing this vague statement, she added, almost as an afterthought, "Although some people do find that their sleep patterns change."

Well, maybe my sleep patterns will change in a positive way and I will finally be able to fall asleep! I thought hopefully. Little did I know that the next few days would involve anything but that wishful thought. I suddenly noticed that Dr. Carmia had exited the room and was already click-clacking down the paneled corridor. Following her sheepishly, I again averted my eyes from anyone in the area, just in case there was someone there whom I knew. Upon reaching the front desk, Dr. Carmia handed my file to the receptionist and, after a cool handshake and a crisp goodbye to me, she was on to her next patient. I quickly scheduled my follow-up appointment, paid the significant bill, and headed towards the exit.

Before I knew it, I was back in my car, riding home with the crumpled prescription in my hand. The last hour had felt like a weird dream to me. But that little white slip of paper with its indecipherable scrawl was proof that it was not a dream. I felt flat and dazed. *Okay,* I told myself, *you took that leap and saw a professional; be proud of yourself for being so mature!* But even with my little pep talk, I felt no sense of pride, nor any sense of catharsis. I wondered once again if things would ever change, uncertain if this quirky doctor and her "magical" pills would do the trick.

I passed by the pharmacy that we used and was about to go in to fill the prescription, when a disturbing thought crossed my mind: *What if someone I know sees me filling this prescription? What if the pharmacist says the drug name aloud and everyone will hear? What if they will look at me as the next "case"?* Chickening out at the last minute, I instead rushed home and begged Baruch to go fill the prescription for me.

With an irritated sigh, he took the paper and headed out to the car. I felt bad for my husband. His nerves were becoming increasingly frayed by the additional burdens placed on him during these tumultuous days. Baruch was a very good person, but he was just that—a person, not an angel. And, like any human being in such a situation, his endurance level was growing weaker with the tremendous pressure he was under.

Between car pools, mortgage bills, job concerns, and family commitments, our life was not as simple as it used to be. Baruch tried to be as helpful as he could, but I noticed a sense of frustration as he assisted me during those hard times. All he wanted was to have his capable wife back—not this withdrawn and dependent woman whom I was becoming. I felt like the lowest of the low as his navy mini-van pulled out of the driveway with a squeal. The noise seemed to reflect Baruch's unspoken cry of annoyance and anger. I felt very guilty for making him do all this extra work because of my shame and insecurity.

When he returned a little while later with the small white paper bag containing an orange medicine bottle, I was full of apologies. "I'm sorry, Baruch. I know how hard this is for you. Please forgive me for my immaturity." I looked at him contritely, and then added, "And for wasting your time and energy."

Baruch shrugged and waved his hand as if he was waving the whole issue aside. "Forget about it, Shoshanah. But do me a favor and don't read the paper listing the possible side effects of this medicine. I don't think that it will do you any good." At his words, I instinctively glanced at the paper attached to the white pharmacy bag, my curiosity aroused. But in deference to Baruch, I allowed him to rip the paper off and discard it, without saying a word.

Before I could lose my courage, I took the bag from Baruch. Opening the small medicine bottle inside, I saw that it was filled with tiny blue tablets. I picked one up, glancing at it warily, then held it up for a closer look. Could it be that this innocent-looking pill harbored enough power to help regulate my anguished mental state? Could it really stop me from "losing it" and going over the infamous "edge"? It just didn't seem feasible. *Probably just some wishful thinking,* I concluded wearily. Yet there was no way of knowing until I tried. And trying was my last resort right now. I knew, from the intuitive wisdom which lies deep within every woman's heart, that this was the form of *hishtadlus*–the human effort that G-d expected of me right now, though every fiber of my being was screaming in fear and resistance.

For every fiber of my being was opposed to this step, opposed to crossing this societal-placed boundary that differentiated between so-called "normal" people, and those who people gabbed about in hushed whispers, saying things like, "You know why things are happening like that in Mrs. So-and-so's home? She's not all there… you know, she's on medication…"—with the innuendo and tone of voice making it quite obvious which type of medication was meant.

And the possible side effects from which Baruch was trying to shield me? Dr. Carmia did not specifically warn me about them, so they were probably uncommon. Yet, as improbable as they were, I was still very frightened. Would I become the zoned-out, glassy-eyed individual one sees at the subway stations? One of the sad-looking people who wandered the streets, displaying to the world their misfortune and weak state of mind? There was no way of knowing what the future held, and I was scared.

Taking medication that affected the brain was the hardest bridge I had to cross so far, for the brain is the organ that symbolizes logic and intellect. It symbolizes intelligence and potential. By taking psychiatric medication, I felt that I was smudging these important traits, which define such a huge part of who we are, and defacing them with a thick black marker, making it impossible for them to be a flawless white again.

I was also extremely afraid of putting myself under the influence of something, which would, in a sense, take away an element of my control. I was terrified that the medicine would control me, affecting me in a manner that would lead me to becoming more sluggish, less sharp, less creative, and even robotic. (For the same reason, I had always wondered how people could let themselves drink alcoholic beverages to the point of intoxication, thus losing all control and inhibitions. I knew that even if it were in my culture to drink, I still would never pick up a glass, for fear of losing my prized sense of control.)

Being a person who so craved to have control, taking this medication was an excruciating step for me. But I knew that I had to do it. Yes, I was frightened to take the plunge, but I was ready for it. I think that I was finally realizing, with my newfound maturity, that people are merely pawns in G-d's hands; that we are *not*, and *were never*, in control of our lives. The most we can ever do are the acts of proper *hishtadlus* in all areas—whether we are comfortable with those acts of effort or not. And so, with one last tearful prayer heavenward for a quick recovery, I placed the little blue tablet on my quivering tongue. Fully aware that after this, there was no going back, I swallowed the pill.

Chapter Ten

"It's not working!" I cried frantically to Baruch a week later, hysteria and panic in my voice. I was faithfully taking the Zoloft each day and yet not only was I not feeling better, but I was becoming more and more agitated with each passing day. The panic symptoms had increased and I constantly felt like I could not breathe properly. My heart would race in middle of the night and I often experienced a "buzzy" feeling, as if I were slightly drunk. I was terrified and truly felt as if I were at the end of my rope. If the medicine could not help me, then what could?

Baruch tried to reassure me that it takes time for medicine to take effect, but I was in no frame of mind to listen. He patiently took me out for a walk while a teenaged neighbor watched our confused children. We walked to a nearby park, where I sat down on a brown wooden bench and promptly burst into a fresh torrent of tears. I was so overwhelmed by my emotions that I did not even care who saw me in my sorry state. "Baruch," I choked out in a voice so broken that I couldn't believe it was emanating from me, "I cannot go on anymore. I've suffered enough. Now no one can say that I haven't tried all my options. I've gone down the last route and have taken the medicine, and for what reason? To feel worse?" I cried out bitterly.

"Please help me, somebody, please help me," I cried out softly, my soul in deep distress. "I just can't go on anymore. There is no more hope for me." I suddenly looked into Baruch's worried eyes, and said in all sincerity and with great conviction, "Give them away."

"Give who away?" he asked me quizzically.

"Give the children away. I can't take care of them anymore, and they deserve a normal life. They deserve a calm environment and a turmoil-free home. I can't give it to them anymore," I said bitterly, my breath coming in ragged gasps.

Baruch nervously tried to tell me to stop saying such nonsense, but at that critical point of my torturous journey, I was dead serious. So great was my internal distress that I negated the close relationship I had with my children, the wonderful care they had received since their births, and their intrinsic need and love for me. "I was never cut out to be a mother," I continued, "and I shouldn't have gotten married, because I am ruining your life, too!" And with that realization, I began to sob and sob, my body shaking and heaving uncontrollably. Baruch sat there helplessly. He, too, felt that we had exhausted all of our options. What were we to do next?

Feeling the buzzy adrenaline coursing through me again at full speed, I abruptly got up and began to pace around the grassy area by the bench. Baruch joined me and tentatively said, "Let's call back Dr. Carmia and ask her what to do next." Clinging to this last straw, I hastily agreed, and we headed back home. I tried to inhale the fresh air around me slowly, but kept on feeling that tight ring around my neck and that oxygen-deprived sensation.

When we arrived home, I tremulously dialed Dr. Carmia's phone number, but to my great distress, her office was closed for the day. All I was given was an emergency number on the answering machine. "Should I call it?" I whispered to Baruch.

"I think so," he answered gravely. "You seem really upset—and I don't know what to do anymore," he admitted weakly.

So, feeling very ashamed yet desperate, I called and left an urgent message about my sky-rocketing panic symptoms. I asked for an immediate return call, as I did not know if what I was experiencing was a negative side effect of the medication, and was not sure what to do next. Then Baruch and I anxiously sat and waited for the doctor to call me back, as her message indicated that she would do so within an hour of receiving a call. But the call for which I was waiting so desperately never did come that entire, terrible Sunday afternoon.

In fact, the doctor never called back until the following morning, after another whole sleepless night of pure suffering and agony...A night where I watched the sky turn from the deepest and darkest shade of black to the lightest shade of blue and wondered if life was worth living anymore...A night where I begged Baruch to forgive me for destroying his life...A torturous night where my pure and innocent children fell asleep fully clothed on the floor of their rooms, where they had drifted off into a restless slumber as they listened to my muffled cries from the next room...A night where Baruch had to feed our newborn son every feeding as I was too exhausted and overwhelmed to even prepare a bottle...

And so, when the phone call did come at precisely 9:00 Monday morning, I practically grabbed the receiver off the hook, so desperate was I to talk to the doctor, and so angry that I had to wait so long in my distraught state. To my utter amazement, she began the conversation by berating me in her crisp and professional voice: "Mrs. Kagan, my emergency line is not to be called unless there is an urgent situation at hand. I do not appreciate being paged on a Sunday afternoon for a routine question about general side effects. Now to answer your question," she continued primly, as inwardly I silently screamed, *"My family is falling apart and I'm about to crack. Does that not qualify as an urgent situation?!"*

"You need to wait six to eight weeks for the medication to work, as I explained to you in the office," she said in an impatient tone of voice.

"But I can't wait," I whispered hoarsely. "I need to sleep. I feel like I can't breathe, and why am I feeling worse?"

Dr. Carmia cut me off and said, "I can prescribe you a sedative to help you relax, and move your follow-up appointment from six weeks to four weeks." And with that, she took down my pharmacy's number and swiftly ended the conversation. I was left holding the phone in a daze.

There were no words of comfort or reassurance, no words of explanation as to why I was feeling worse. I truly felt like a specimen under Dr. Carmia's scientific microscope—not like a human being, who, in such distress, felt that life was not worth living anymore.

In a shocked and dazed voice, I filled Baruch in on my three-minute conversation with the doctor. Baruch was enraged. "She probably treats her dog better than her patients!" he said, as I gingerly sat on the edge of the couch, my head in my arms.

Take another medication? I had been so very scared of taking medication to begin with, and for good reason, after what was happening to me now. And here the doctor was, recommending another unknown drug, some kind of sedative—"to help you relax". Who knew how I would react to that?

Baruch seemed to be feeling the same way. He suddenly stood up, a new maturity and resolve apparent on his face. "We are going to find another doctor to talk to. Somebody who will be kind and caring and treat his or her patients like the people they are." With that, he left the room and headed to his small study, where I could hear him talking on the phone. As for me, I lay down on the couch, the room spinning around me. I had reached a point of apathy. My eyes drifted off on their own accord and I fell into a fitful and confused slumber.

Within an hour, Baruch had gotten the name of a new psychiatrist. He had called Dr. Gupta, my OB-GYN, at her busy office, and had gotten hold of her with persistence. Explaining what was going on, he asked for advice. Dr. Gupta grasped the severity of the situation and gave him the number of a local psychiatrist to whom she referred patients suffering from PPD. She was appalled that I had not informed her of my symptoms and that I had tried to seek help on my own. She explained that PPD is a specific women's health issue for which a psychiatrist needs to be specifically trained in order to properly treat; and not all psychiatrists fell into that category. Baruch tried to explain my line of reasoning—how ashamed I was to admit to anything—but she cut him off abruptly, telling him that there was no need for shame and he would not believe how common this ailment is.

Baruch called the new doctor whom Dr. Gupta had recommended, as I sat on the couch and rocked a fretful Ezzy in his infant seat. Thank G-d, the other kids were in school, thanks to Baruch's help that morning. *Baruch is missing a day of work*, I suddenly realized through the fog that enveloped me. I had completely lost track of our family's regular schedule throughout this awful time.

I heard Baruch speak to the psychiatrist, a Dr. Kostner, and explain our predicament to her. I watched him silently, my heart in my throat. Suddenly, he held out the phone to me and, covering the mouthpiece, whispered, "She wants to talk to you."

Numbly, I took the phone and put it by my ear. "Hello," I said hesitantly.

A warm and caring voice answered me, so unlike the clipped and cool voice of Dr. Carmia. "Hello, Mrs. Kagan. This is Dr. Kostner. I understand that you are not feeling very well."

"Not really," I said softly, and my voice began to break in response to the doctor's caring voice. "I feel very sick. I need to be well for my children…" I stopped abruptly, too choked up to continue.

Dr. Kostner proceeded to tell me that although she was booked solid for the next two weeks, her next patient for that day had cancelled, and if I could be in her office within a half hour, she could see me then.

Even in my state of misery, I felt a current run through me as I recognized the tremendous Divine providence going on here. Had we contacted Dr. Kostner even an hour later, I would've had to wait weeks for an appointment with her. G-d had arranged for us to call exactly at a time when Dr. Kostner had a free hour to spare. Somehow, I instinctively felt that Dr. Kostner would be the right person, that she would be able to help me, and I immediately accepted the appointment. Feeling a faint ray of hope stirring within me, I ran out to the car, leaving Baruch holding sweet little Ezzy. Baruch couldn't come with me, as Moshe Dovid would be returning from his half-day nursery program soon and would need supervision.

As I hastily pulled out of the driveway, I said to Baruch impassionedly, "Please pray for me." Baruch nodded gravely and warned me to drive extremely carefully, being that I was in such an exhausted state. Gripping the steering wheel with shaking hands, I then drove off to meet Dr. Kostner. Was my harrowing journey perhaps about to take a turn for the better?

Dr. Kostner indeed proved to be the Heaven-sent doctor that I needed. As soon as I entered her cozy pastel-blue office with its myriad of trinkets displayed, I felt calmer. Dr. Kostner was a middle-aged woman with dark brown hair and deep blue eyes, which exuded both scholarship and warmth. She asked me many questions about my history and present symptoms. She then took the time to explain to me that for someone suffering from PPD with primary anxious symptoms and secondary depressive ones, like me, she did not feel that Zoloft was the proper drug.

"Zoloft is an activating kind of drug," Dr. Kostner explained. "It's meant to arouse one out of a subdued, depressive state. Since you are feeling the opposite of subdued, with all your adrenaline-racing symptoms, you need to take something with a more calming quality." She then proceeded to switch me to a similar yet more appropriate anti-depressant, called Celexa. She also promptly prescribed for me a strong tranquilizer/sleeping pill, which she instructed that I take religiously for the next few weeks, even if I needed to hire a baby night nurse for Ezzy.

The reason why my anxiety and emotional state was so out of whack, she told me, was because my sleeping cycle was so off-kilter. And after a while of lack of sleep, she continued patiently, the nervous system can't handle it and will begin to mimic psychiatric symptoms.

Though I was terrified of taking any more pills, I felt that I could trust this doctor. Even in my confused state, I could see that she was sharp, on the ball, and displayed true human compassion and caring. I also trusted Dr. Gupta, who had referred me to this new doctor, and therefore my fears were somewhat allayed.

Dr. Kostner also instructed me to call her at any time, even at night, with any concerns that might arise. She and her colleague were on hand at all times, and one of them would return the call immediately. *What a stark contrast to Dr. Carmia*, I thought to myself as I listened to the doctor's professional yet caring voice. I was also to have a follow-up visit in two weeks to see how the medications were working.

As I left Dr. Kostner's office, the faint glimmer of hope in my broken heart began to shine even brighter. Clasping the prescription in my hand, I dared to believe that perhaps there *was* hope for me after all...

Chapter Eleven

I woke up early the next morning, feeling slightly disoriented. And then with a flash, I remembered the events of yesterday. I couldn't believe it–the sleeping pill had worked! I had slept! I had slept! My immense relief knew no bounds as I slowly got up from bed. I had slept for seven hours straight, thanks to Baruch, who had given the baby his middle-of-the-night feeding. I felt a sense of calm running through me, sort of like a rush of warm, soothing energy. Like the feeling one has holding a toasty warm mug of hot cocoa on a freezing winter day. The sedative was at work, I realized. My gratitude upon realization of this fact was enormous. Though I was still shaky and weak, I was feeling ten times better than I had felt a mere twenty-four hours ago. What a miracle that I had gotten to speak to Dr. Kostner the day before! Remembering the traumatic events of yesterday morning, I shuddered to think about what state of mind I would have been in without the medicine to relax me and help me sleep.

That Tuesday I spent the day in suspense. Would this feeling of calmness last? Would I momentarily revert back to that feeling of indescribable doom that I had felt the day before? I also frequently wondered if I appeared zombie-like to the world. Was it evident that I had taken a tranquilizer? Would I have to stay on sedatives for the rest of my life? Was it a cop-out? Had I won the battle, yet lost the war?

These thoughts crossed my mind continuously and scared me,

but my reaction to them did not cause the intense physical symptoms that I had been fighting for so long. The drug I had taken was powerful, I realized, and very effective. Looking in the mirror, I tried to surmise if I appeared different, if I looked spaced-out. Would I see a green-haired, wild-eyed, grotesque monster with horns, holding a florescent sign that boldly stated, "I take psychiatric medicine"?

I saw my reflection staring back at me: a young woman in the prime of life whose frightened-looking hazel eyes gave the impression that she had the weight of the world on her shoulders. But spacey? "Zoned out"? Disassociated from the world? Green-haired and wild-eyed? No, I concluded with relief. I still looked like me, the same 'me' who I had known for the past twenty-nine years.

I recall going through that day on eggshells. I was able to attend to the kids properly and have calm and meaningful conversations with Baruch. Yet the up-and-down emotional roller coaster of the past few weeks had taken their toll on my trust in everything, including the medicines I was now taking. Was I really on the road back to health and stability? Was that really all it took, a simple miniscule tranquilizer to help me sleep? Was there more to it? Would I spiral backwards if I would stop taking medication? I looked to Baruch for these answers, as if he possessed more knowledge on the subject than me, which of course he did not. He gently advised me to take it one step at a time, reassuring me again and again that he would stand behind me all the way. My wonderful and wise husband succeeded in calming my fears, and for the moment, I was able to relax.

A good night's sleep had definitely jump-started my road to recovery, yet I was still far from better. The overwhelming emotions were still present, though they were thankfully being held in check by the nightly sedative that I was taking. Like it or not, I would have to wait a good six to eight weeks to really feel the true benefits of the new anti-depressant that I had been prescribed.

A few days passed. Oh, how my mindset had changed! I now

treasured and appreciated taking the pills each night. I saw the mercy of G-d in them, as they led me into a deep sleep and allowed me to recharge and forget my predicament for a good seven hours. Yet, as I began each new day, I couldn't help but wonder and doubt if things would ever return to normal, really normal—when I would be my old self again. Each time my thoughts strayed in this direction, I firmly reminded myself to be patient and not make any final assumptions until a full eight weeks had passed.

During the following week, I was glancing through a Jewish periodical when a "letter to the editor" caught my attention, as it was speaking about a reader's struggle with anxiety and depression. She was writing the letter to inform the Orthodox community about a wonderful secular audio/visual self-help program offered by The Midwest Center for Stress and Anxiety. The program was called "Attacking Anxiety and Depression". She claimed that it was true to Torah ideology and had helped her a great deal. My curiosity piqued, I spontaneously called the contact number that had been included in the letter and ordered the kit. I then promptly forgot about it and waited earnestly for the Celexa to kick in and start working, while faithfully continuing in the interim to take my nightly sleeping pill/tranquilizer. Little did I know that I had just invested in a purchase which would prove to be a crucial key in my recovery, and of equal importance to the medication.

The bell rang one morning as I was washing the dishes. *Who could that be?* I wondered as I put down the dish soap and dried my wet hands. It was 11:00 A.M. on a regular Thursday morning—not exactly a time for one to receive visitors. I headed to the front door and peeked through the peephole. I saw the image of a tall U.P.S. worker walking towards his brown delivery truck. *Oh*, I realized woodenly. *I must have gotten that package that I ordered from the Midwest Center for Stress and Anxiety.*

Opening the door and examining the large parcel, I realized that my assumption was correct. Warily, I looked at it and shook my head. I was resigned to just wait for the anti-depressant to take full effect. *But I already spent the money on this,* I thought to myself. *I guess I might as well listen to some of the CDs and look through the accompanying reading material.*

The house was quiet and I was relatively calm. I slipped the CD labeled "Relaxation" into our CD player and pressed "play". The CD began: "You and I are about to go on an amazing journey..."

The speaker continued by instructing the listener to lie down in a comfortable place. "Close your eyes. Feel your abdomen rise and fall with each steady breath... Count with me: Breathe in, one, two; breathe out, one, two, three, four... Feel a warm, embracing light spreading through your limbs, releasing the tension. Let go. Let go of the fear... Let go of the sadness... Let go of the anger... You are relaxed; you are content; you are safe... Picture yourself in a lush green pasture surrounded by magnificent foliage... Rainbow-colored wildflowers surround you, and the breathtaking horizon beckons you... You are awed by the beauty around you, so thankful to be a part of this wondrous world... You feel a spirit of strength permeating your being... You feel grateful, humble, spiritual... You are filled with a sense of mission and a spirit of vitality... Greatness lies within you, and you are ready to share it... You are ready to embrace the world with all its beauty and potential, and you are strong enough to face its challenges... You feel yourself healing step by step... You are strong; you are capable... You feel a positive energy within you, spreading its rays to those around you... You have so much to share, so much good to offer... You are happy; you are content; you are so grateful to be alive... Life is good..."

Intrigued by the speaker's warm, compassionate and knowledgeable voice, I found myself moved to tears by what she was saying. I realized that the speaker was none other than Lucinda Basset, CEO of the Midwest Center for Stress and Anxiety, who herself had experienced severe anxiety and depression as a young adult. Against the odds, she had overcome her condition, and had made it her mission in life to help the thousands of other anxiety victims who were suffering in anguished silence to do the same.

So taken was I by her kind and down-to-earth style and sincere message, that I resolved to go through the fifteen-week-program properly. It was a commitment, I realized, but, as I told myself, it could only help.

It could *only help*? What an understatement! During the next fifteen weeks, I learned more about my "condition" and about myself than ever before. I learned that people who struggle from anxiety and depression are usually intelligent, analytical, and highly creative individuals who are channeling their G-d-given strengths inward and subconsciously seeking to reach a perfection that is impossible to maintain. I learned that although I appeared to the public as a happy and easygoing person, inwardly I was the consummate people-pleaser, always afraid of losing favor in others' eyes and of thereby losing my status, because approval meant so much to my fragile ego.

I learned how my obsessive, scary thoughts were my mind's way of distracting me from the overwhelming events going on in my life. Due to my creative flair, the thoughts were quite spicy—yet they were the furthest thing from reality. The fact that I was actually *afraid* of the thoughts was the biggest indicator that I'd never act upon them, and that they were nothing but, plain and simple, some over-imaginative thoughts, without one drop of authenticity to them! I also learned that to get rid of the thoughts, I would have to forego my craving for a sense of total control—which, I learned, was an impossibility anyway—and learn to live with the level of uncertainty that all human beings face.

I also learned that anxiety and depression are genetic predispositions that are prevalent in countless families and experienced by people from all spectrums of life and across the socio-economic sphere. I learned about the gift and role of medication; how it is, in most cases, an adjunct and not a cure. True healing comes when one challenges his inner critique and reprograms himself with healthy beliefs.

I listened to countless other deep-thinking, intelligent, and often humorous people who kindly shared their experiences on CD, in order to give their support to those participating in the program. I listened, learned, and slowly began to internalize the messages.

The program took great concentration and effort. It effectively took the place of going to an experienced therapist, who in essence tries to teach the same skills to his or her clients. Although at this point I had gotten over the stigma of that approach, I could not consider that option due to monetary and time constraints. I also knew my personality and circumstances. I had always been somewhat of an independent thinker and liked to do things on my own turf and timetable. I was motivated by self-improvement done on a private scale, although I did utilize the group support offered on the CDs. I knew that these personality traits would help me to complete this program, where accountability is the onus of the user.

I also was fully aware—and very thankful—that my husband was a supportive ally on my quest to recovery. Without his interest and encouragement, I could not have done it. Looking back in hindsight, I am awed at the kindness of G-d, that He sent me a program so completely tailor-made to my strengths and circumstances. I realize that every person's temperament and family support system is different. Some people would find such a do-it-yourself approach unfeasible and ineffective. They may benefit from talking one-on-one with a trained mental health professional who can guide them in depth and monitor their progress. Especially if one does not have support from his or her spouse and/or family, an encouraging therapist may make all the difference in one's recovery.

Most importantly, I realized that although the medication I took was a lifesaver during that critical point in my journey, *it was only in conjunction with the techniques that I learned and internalized that I was able to heal fully.* The medication gave me the floor back to stand on, by effectively addressing the chemical imbalance present, as I reprogrammed my mind with healthy beliefs and discarded the old, faulty ones that had helped trigger my PPD episodes.

Week after week, I pored over the workbooks provided and listened to the CD's. I did the prescribed homework and learned how to "face my fears" in a variety of ways. The biological origin of depression and anxiety was discussed, and steps to overcome panic attacks were taught. Underlying issues such as perfectionism, lack of healthy assertiveness, and misplaced anger were spoken about in great detail. And above all, the theme of learning to tame one's negative inner critic and take charge of empowering oneself with positive thoughts was interspersed throughout all the lessons. Another major theme that was constantly stressed was that medicine for anxiety and depression is very appropriate at the right times and for the right reasons; whether it is needed for a few months or for a lifetime. However, the truest sense of recovery and relief is felt when one internalizes the powerful messages that negate his inner critic, helping him to see the positive and to live life in the precious present moment.

And so those precarious weeks passed. True to Dr. Kostner's words, the medication did eventually "kick in" and take effect. I began to feel emotionally lighter, more optimistic and more clearheaded. I thanked G-d daily for the blessing of these pills and for their valuable help in my recovery. And as unbelievable as it sounds, I reached a point where I was able to giggle at the memory of how frightened I used to be of them. The pills did not diminish my essence, as I had been so afraid that they would; they simply helped me to relax and lifted that horrible fog of despair that had enveloped me so tightly. They also effectively broke the chain of obsessive thoughts that had tormented me for so long. For the first time, I was able to objectively recognize how ridiculous and farfetched these thoughts were, and how they posed no real threat. Once I stopped being afraid of them, they ceased to bother me, and consequently became less and less frequent.

The medication also did not induce me into a state of unnatural happiness, as I worried it might do. It simply took off the edge and eased my symptoms, so that I could focus on recovering. And my greatest fear, that everyone would take one look at me and "know" that I was on medication, was completely unfounded. The medications used for treating anxiety and depression do not change one's personality; they simply help the person relax. I don't think anyone in their wildest dreams would have ever suspected that outgoing and personable Shoshanah Kagan, of "play-dough and homemade chocolate-chip cookie mommy" fame, was taking medication for depression and anxiety. And even if by some chance someone did suspect it—so what! I knew I was doing the right thing.

It took a long time and a lot of patience on my part, but eventually I felt like myself again. Although I had long ago been weaned off the tranquilizers as my sleep cycle became more regular, I was instructed by Dr. Kostner to stay on the anti-depressant for a full year under her supervision in order to prevent a relapse. I agreed wholeheartedly, and eagerly moved on with my life.

Thank G-d, the nightmare was finally over.

Chapter Twelve

"Ma Ma Ma Ma!" Little Ezzy gurgled happily in his white crib. I opened the door to his cheery yellow bedroom, and Ezzy squealed with delight. His happiness upon seeing me was written all over his cherubic face. His sky-blue eyes shone and his impish face was wreathed with the most magnificent smile beneath his soft brown curls.

I scooped nineteen-month-old Ezzy out of his crib and held him close to me. Then I walked with him to the large bay window in our living room. There we stood together, Ezzy and I, looking out at the horizon set before us on this cloudy and crisp, early autumn morning.

I felt Ezzy's soft and chubby hands patting my cheeks and pressing my nose. My little clown just loved it when I said, "Beep beep" in response, and he erupted into appreciative giggles. "Oh, Ezzy," I said, hugging his warm body, "I love you so much!" I proceeded to change and dress him, and then took him to the kitchen and placed him in his red and white high chair located in the corner of our cozy tan kitchen.

As he sat there, scooping up his beloved Cheerios with his little fingers, I contemplated how much life had changed for us in the past year and a half. Just as Ezzy had grown from the frail newborn he used to be, to the strong and solid toddler he was now, I, too, had grown. Yet my growth was a much more indiscernible one, invisible to the physical eye, although glaring to the spiritual soul.

I had grown in the way that I viewed life and the world around me. No longer would I ever take for granted the magnificent and wonderful gift of mental health. I had come to realize that just as we ask G-d, and thank Him, for the use of our limbs and organs, so, too, we need to ask and thank Him for the wondrous gift of waking up each morning with our faculties intact.

No more would I ever feel that being emotionally and mentally stable is a birthright; something to be expected, without recognition or appreciation. No, my worldview had changed, and I had begun thanking G-d with every fiber of my being and from the deepest depths of my soul for every single one of the myriads of kindnesses that He does. The magnificent ability to drift off into a deep and restful slumber with ease, and awake the next morning recharged and with the emotional strength and stamina needed to face the coming day. The gift of having a healthy appetite for food and drink, and the ability to partake of them daily without a lump in one's throat accompanying each swallow.

And no longer would I take for granted the awesome gift of a clear head and an unburdened heart; a head that could make decisions and problem-solve throughout the day with alacrity, and a heart that felt light and joyful as it embraced the challenges and circumstances of life with optimism.

Yes, I was fully cognizant of the positive transformation which had emerged as a result of my regained mental health, and I truly felt as if I had been given a second chance at life. And with this second chance, I had the opportunity to live through the eyes of someone who had emerged from the blackest hole that exists in this world. A hole where the usual coping tools of logic and faith are useless, as they are the very objects under vicious attack by a very real and frightening enemy named despair.

It is here, in this deep dark hole, that feelings of intense isolation quickly morph into existential angst. One suddenly becomes acutely aware of the vastness of the cosmos and how seemingly insignificant he or she is. Without the feeling of security that comes from recognizing the spiritual anchors holding up the universe, all seems pointless and futile. This feeling of no purpose to one's existence, no rhyme or reason to life, is sheer torture to the sufferer. And the religious answers generally used to counteract this feeling are of no help, as the dark veil of depression mercilessly obscures one's spiritual vision and constricts the soul.

In this deep pit of suffering, the afflicted one begins to truly understand the expression "empty shell", for that is essentially what he or she has become. Although one's physical body may be hale and hearty, the spark of light within has been extinguished. Going through the motions of everyday life requires much effort and appears to be a mocking sham. Can there be a deeper pain in the world than to feel as if one's life truly has no purpose?

And so, when I now recognize one who is in emotional pain, a flood of feelings rush through me. Firstly, I feel an overwhelming rush of compassion for this suffering human being. No one wants to be in such a sorry state, and no genuine and honest soul is putting on a show for attention. Emotional pain is real and very profound. I recognize that the person is trudging through a claustrophobic tunnel with seemingly no end in sight.

My sensitivity radar has been thoroughly fine-tuned, and no longer do I try to avoid these people and attempt to brush past them when I see them. I look them straight in the eye and smile kindly, whether they acknowledge me or not. I mentally wish them well, and offer up a silent prayer for them from the bottom of my heart that they should be blessed to find a healthy way out of the internal maze in which they find themselves trapped. I realize that each of these people, no matter how sorry-looking he or she may appear to be on the outside, has an ethereal soul deep within.

I have come to recognize how truly dependent we are on G-d. It is not hard for the Creator of the world, the most powerful King, to crank our intricately formed brains and hearts and leave us lurching in the dark. We are not in total control of our mental and emotional abilities and functions, although we may delude ourselves to believe otherwise. And so, I have come to learn that the best sense of control there exists, is, ironically, *to give up some control* and yield to G-d. By doing this, we are putting our trust and hope in G-d to guide us and lead us through the journeys that we must travel. The most we can do is put in our personal effort, with hearts full of hope that we will be led in the right direction.

About effort—boy, have I learned about effort! I have come to realize that effort is about doing whatever actions need to be done, whether we want to do them or not. I am now aware that the medication that I dreaded, although I so desperately needed it, was actually a concrete manifestation of G-d's glory and kindness disguised in a little pill: a blessing from above, just like the manna in the desert. I thank G-d for bringing to the world this healing salvation to help us navigate treacherous waters when stormy weather arrives. Indeed, when used with proper care, these medications are a figurative life jacket to those needing them.

My mind raced back to my emotional meeting with Rabbi Feld so many years before. *"One day, you'll look back at this period in your life and you'll be surprised at how you weathered this storm. In fact, you'll see that there was even some good that came out of it,"* Rabbi Feld had said to me. It had been hard for me to believe his words then, yet here I was, presently recalling his words and realizing how very true they were! Yes, much good *had* come from my whole painful experience. For by experiencing and living through emotional illness, I had emerged from a cocoon of narrow-minded naiveté, in which I'd never thought twice about being condescending and passing judgment on others who seemed emotionally "weak" in my eyes, and had been given new wings to fly above this negativity and enter an atmosphere of total acceptance, reality, and true faith. I had emerged stronger and more confident in myself, and had metamorphosed into a more humble and sensitive servant of G-d.

In short, I have been taught how to live life the way it is meant to be lived: with joy and gratitude for each new day, and trust in the

Almighty to guide me through it. *Yes, Rabbi Feld, you were right after all. It has taken me a long time to realize the truth in your words, but I now realize that my painful experience has been for the good.*

I now wake up each morning with a sense of appreciation and purpose. Every new day of life heralds a chance to utilize my G-d-given gifts and change the world! No, I am not leading countries or building corporations. I am molding precious souls that have been entrusted to me from Above. I am taking fragile egos, raw talents and pure potential, and helping my innocent children develop into unique individuals.

To know that I am playing my part in my children's lives with the gift of a clear and healthy mind and heart arouses great joy within me. After having suffered from Postpartum Depression, I now understand what a tremendous gift from G-d this is. No, like everyone else in this world, I don't know what tomorrow will bring, but my experiences have truly taught me to *live life in the present* and appreciate the seemingly small things. I now recognize that if I wait for happiness and satisfaction to greet me without any effort on my part, the wait might be a long and interminable one.

Bang! The clang of Ezzy's sippy cup as it fell down on the floor interrupted my reverie. I picked up the purple cup and gave it to him—and he promptly threw it down again with that irresistible dimpled grin of his! Hearing the sounds of Avrami, Devorah, and Moshe Dovid stirring upstairs, I readied myself for another busy morning of brushing hair, pouring milk, and writing mitzvah notes. I rolled up my sleeves and headed towards the stairs. On the way, I took another quick peek out the bay window at the now glorious, early morning sky.

The sky had changed from the murky gray it had been an hour ago, to a deep indigo blue. The angry-looking gray clouds had transformed themselves into puffy white balls of cotton gently sailing by. And the sun—that deep ball of golden fire—lit up the world with a mesmerizing radiance. Spreading its illuminating rays in all directions, it reminded me of the passion within us all to rectify ourselves, and the world in which we live.

My heart swelled with joy at the sight, and I reveled in the delight of precious life and its remarkable beauty. And just as it is easier to rejoice in the light and deep warmth of the glorious sun after the long and dark night, so I was able to appreciate the newfound light in my soul after my experience with darkness.

"Mommy!" Devorah called to me.

I left the bay window and bounded up the stairs. No time to dawdle—the school bus would be here soon!

"I'm coming, Devorah!" I called up to my six-year-old daughter. I reached her room and opened the door. "Mommy is here for you," I said with a heart full of gratitude. "Thank G-d, Mommy is here for you."

The Land of Acceptance

Dear Reader,

By reading this book, you have taken the first step of an amazing journey—a journey of strength and bravery that will lead you from a frightening, deserted, and parched island to a populated, scenic, seaside land. The coast brimming with endless white sand, whispering palm trees, and crystal-blue rolling waves is dotted by its many inhabitants. These inhabitants all have warm hearts, kind smiles and outstretched hands, and they are ready to offer their assistance to all newcomers.

Many of these people have arrived here after the same harrowing journey on which you are about to embark. They, too, had to make that initial leap into the frigid waters surrounding the deserted isle. Clutching a small life preserver labeled "hope", they held on tightly as the stormy waters tossed and turned them for what seemed like an eternity, leaving the travelers shaky and so very cold.

Finally, when they felt like they could bear it no longer, the high tide began to recede and the waves became more gentle and soothing. The bright sun began to emerge from the murky horizon. Before their very eyes, a tentative shoreline began to materialize. It was the land that the voyagers had worked so hard to reach. It was the land of acceptance.

It is here, in this glorious sun-kissed land, that one can be free to be just as His Creator had fashioned him to be. No one is judgmental in this place. All emotional make-ups and personalities are accepted. The only code of law to be followed is the Divine one given from Above.

The residents of this Land of Acceptance do just that—accept themselves and those around them unconditionally and with great love. They try to emulate G-d, Who accepts all of His beloved children with all their inner complexities and human foibles. Within this spirit of belonging, the dwellers, who have each taken whatever individual steps are needed for their health, have internalized a spirit of inner peace and harmony.

And so, dear reader, I implore you to take the plunge and join me, as well as all the other residents of this land. Swim towards us by reaching out for the help you need, if you are suffering from Postpartum Depression and/or related emotional disorders.

Please be aware that the journey will be tough, but know, that the satisfaction that you will feel at its conclusion will be all worth it. For it is here, on the blessed shores of the Land of Acceptance, where one truly learns to accept himself, and ironically, this teaches him to recognize the fathomless well of strength that he has within himself. The magnificent joy that comes with this knowledge lets you know in no uncertain terms that you have moved to the right land. You have truly arrived home.

Baruch's Perspective

Shoshanah asked me to contribute a chapter to this book regarding my experience and perspective as the husband of a wife with postpartum depression. She also thought it would be helpful if I could supply any practical advice for men going through a similar situation. However, when looking back at this period of our lives, I soon realized that writing such a chapter would not be easy. Much of the experience remains loaded with strong emotions, and parts of it I only remember as an overwhelming blur. Giving advice isn't a simple matter either. I don't feel that I passed this test with flying colors, nor am I on the level necessary to give guidance to others. Still, perhaps that is exactly what is needed: an honest portrayal of an average husband's ups and downs in living through such an experience, and an open admission of mistakes and small victories for others to learn from and build upon. Please keep in mind that this chapter is only a supplement to the advice and guidance of the esteemed professionals recorded in the second part of this book; your local mentor and/or competent professional should remain your first choice of consultation in learning to deal with this situation.

When I think of the start of my wife's experience with PPD, I'm reminded of a conversation with a cousin in which he gently poked fun at how people act so formally in certain situations, such as at weddings and organizational dinners. There is an (understandable) reluctance to "just be oneself", for fear of other people's criticism or judgment. That's how it was when Shoshanah had her first bout with PPD. As a couple, the two of us were still "acting" with each other, as all young couples do at the beginning of marriage. Shoshanah was at first too inhibited to tell me about her suffering, while I myself was just transitioning from the newlywed period to being the father of one child and then of two, and I certainly wasn't ready for adjusting to yet another role – that of being the supportive husband of a wife with PPD.

With hardly any warning, my competent and cheerful wife had become moody and anxious, insecure in areas of self-esteem and self-confidence. She stopped sleeping and would dread nighttime; a dark shadow seemed to be etched permanently on her drawn face. Obsessive thoughts would drain her of a tremendous amount of energy; I could see how exhausting this was for her both physically and psychologically. I was full of fear seeing Shoshanah like this; this person was an imposter, a strangely twisted mirror image of my wife. I couldn't understand how such a happy event as the birth of our child could have plunged her into such depths of despair.

Somehow, one thought kept me moving forward, like a beacon in the darkness: The old Shoshanah had to be there somewhere, the Shoshanah I'd gotten to know over the course of the months of our dating, our engagement, our wedding and first year of marriage, the birth of our first child, and beyond. I'd get her back. I'd fix this problem. It would be like building the baby's crib from the manual—at first incomprehensible and frustrating (especially for a guy with two left hands), but after long hours and with patience, no problem. I'd fix this problem, too—alone—and the Shoshanah I'd known would click back into place.

So after a long day studying in yeshivah, I'd come home at suppertime, anticipating a wondrous, magical change. I'd walk in, wanting a hot meal, the kitchen cozy and neat, my wife holding the baby, and both of them smiling beatifically. It was hard for someone with my personality to put away this idealized fantasy in exchange for reality; I wasn't flexible enough with my expectations. I would try to remain calm on the outside, while my inner voice ranted and raged. Surely all of my peers were coming home to the scene I'd imagined! (Hadn't it seemed so on the outside whenever I'd been in their homes?) On some level, I knew Shoshanah had hardly slept. She'd somehow managed going to work and taking care of the baby, but she was barely getting through the day. There were serious hormonal changes affecting her mood and her thinking. But my initial reaction was one of intense frustration—I didn't care. I just wanted things to be the way they'd been earlier on, before this whole PPD situation.

I was tired of the mood shifts. Shoshanah seemed to want to talk a lot about everything, but sometimes she seemed so remote. She didn't want to go to social functions, despite always having had a way of connecting with people and putting them at ease. A fake smile had replaced her real one. Why couldn't she snap out of it and just be happy again?

I soon found myself emotionally and physically exhausted from the ordeal. I understood what Shoshanah was going through to a degree, but started to feel less sympathetic for her. After all, I was going through this, too, wasn't I? I later came to realize that it can be difficult for a man to truly relate to PPD, to his spouse's emotions and feelings in living with this condition.

The need to provide unconditional support for my wife was taking its toll on me. I'd try to build her up (often with platitudes; "It will be good" and "Just try to distract yourself" were two of my favorites), and she'd harshly knock my efforts down. It was hard to realize that it was the PPD and anxiety talking, and not really "her". The condition made Shoshanah genuinely believe that she'd never recover; she really couldn't see a brighter future. I felt helpless, as nothing I said or did seemed to work to "fix" the problem. I didn't appreciate how much I was doing just by my listening to Shoshanah and offering her my sympathy. Instead, I felt inadequate and unimportant.

Other areas were difficult as well. I remember waking up one night, completely disoriented. It was pitch dark and something hard and rounded was poking into my side. As my consciousness grew, I realized what had happened. I'd been rocking the baby, buckled into her infant seat on the floor, for my completely exhausted wife. After a while, I'd drifted off to sleep, still on the floor, and had ended up underneath my bed, a sneaker in close proximity!

Meals, once elaborate and home-cooked, were often no longer possible due to Shoshanah's lack of energy, and cold cereal had to suffice. When Shoshanah's PPD returned and there were more children to rock, feed, hold, etc., the physical burden grew even more.

I began to resent Shoshanah for the chaos that had replaced our formerly calm and cheerful life. Occasionally, I would lash out in frustration and anger. More often, though, I would rage internally instead of screaming. That was my way of dealing with stress and conflict—but such a method can exact an enormous toll on one's physical and emotional health, as I learned from experience. I suffered a lot during this period, feeling both helpless and hopeless. I went from feeling detached and numb to my wife's pain, to feeling hurt and angry beyond words at her attitude and behavior.

Eventually, I realized that what Shoshanah needed from me was a listening ear and reassuring words. My advice didn't have to be amazingly profound. My wife just needed to know that my support would not waver, no matter how long or what means it took for her to recover.

Nevertheless, after Shoshanah's second episode of PPD, I came to realize what a precarious situation we were in. We couldn't do it alone anymore. We had to rely on others for assistance. With the help of G-d, we were able to utilize the valuable resource of a competent mental health professional, once we merited finding the right one.

It was not singlehandedly my responsibility to "fix". A crushing weight was lifted off my shoulders as I shared the burden with other family members and my *rav*, while still remaining a vital component of Shoshanah's recovery process. And change eventually came to be, with the help of G-d, and I found that Shoshanah, as I'd known her, *had* been there all along – we'd merely grown together.

Whenever someone in my wife's family was feeling embarrassed or ashamed about something, for example, speaking in public or coming late to an event through no fault of his or her own, my wife's grandmother, of blessed memory, had a unique response. She was a Holocaust survivor with deep faith, a woman who had a wonderful sharpness and a regal sense of dignity. She would say in Yiddish, "*Far vus shemzich; du hust eppes giganvit?* (Why are you ashamed; did you steal?)" It was a wonderful insight, highlighting when a sense of shame or stigma is called for—and when it is not. Shoshanah and I learned that mental illness is not something for which a person should be ashamed.

I'd like to conclude this chapter with some general guidelines which I hope will be useful to other husbands going through the ordeal of dealing with PPD together with their wives. Certainly, every marriage is different, and every episode of PPD may differ in duration, form, and intensity. The following is what I realized (basically, through trial and error) worked for me, and what I've gleaned from various sources.

1) Establish firmly in your mind the past, future, and present. The past: internalizing the mental image of the person you got to know through dates, engagement, and marriage up until this point. This picture you have of your wife is who she really is – and will be, with G-d's help, in the future. The future: recognizing that the PPD period is a transitory one, a period based on chang-

ing hormonal levels that will eventually return to normal. The future is bright, and can and will be everything you've hoped for and imagined. The present: focusing on getting through this difficult time on a day-by-day basis, while at the same time being prepared to be in it "for the long haul" and reaching out for help.

2) Our nature as men is to look for something concrete to do. The temptation here is to quickly "fix" the problem, when in fact the passage of time is essential for things to level out. This temptation must be channeled into practical ways to help your wife, your family, and yes – yourself.

Often, what may be frustrating is that what seems logical and rational to you, won't seem so to her. "Being firm with her" and ordering her to just "snap out of it" will not work. Trying to empathize by saying something like, "I know what you're going through" won't help, either. Though it is well-intentioned, you *don't* really know what she is going through. So what can and should be said or done; how can you be a supportive spouse?

Your wife likely feels isolated and insecure; to combat these feelings, she needs your sympathy and compassion. She wants to feel it is safe for her to share her thoughts with you – no matter what they are. Talk about the progress she's making and give her positive feedback. Compliment her genuinely. Never compare her with others. With constant repetition, the positive comments you give her are registering, at least on some level.

One of the hardest aspects of dealing with your wife will be her reaction to your support: often, she may not acknowledge your efforts. Occasionally, she will respond with bitterness or even lash out in anger. The source of her emotions is the PPD and the anxiety, depression, and frustration that accompany it. It is not personal. Nevertheless, do not become the punching bag. You can and should calmly but firmly stand up for yourself. Don't blow up; just let your wife know that such comments are not called for, as you are her ally and closest friend in this struggle.

3) It is of vital importance to keep up your closeness as a couple. When "PPD talk" begins to feel obsessive, switch to speaking about other things, such as common interests and daily experiences. Eat out, go shopping, just take a stroll around the block – keep it light! Your wife may feel compelled to constantly think and talk about her condition. Keep her away from compulsive fixes like this. Encourage her to do activities that you know she really enjoys, even if now she feels that she won't enjoy them. The goal here is distraction – with a gentle push.

4) During this critical period, it is imperative that you take care of your own health, too. Take time for yourself. Find healthy and appropriate outlets, and use them wisely and without guilt. Most of all, know that you cannot do this all alone. You need to utilize the appropriate resources.

5) As much as possible, educate yourself about PPD. The more you know about the ways the condition can manifest, the brain chemistry and hormones behind it all, as well as how common it is, the more reassured and prepared you will be to cope with this development. We often fear an unknown quality and its accompanying stigma much more than the condition or situation itself.

6) Reach out to your support system. Speak to a mentor and to a qualified mental health professional in confidence. If you are uncomfortable about sharing and discussing everything in detail, generalize that you are having trouble with a situation in your home life. It is important to be as honest and open as possible, so that your mentor/advisor can gauge the seriousness of the situation and guide you in his response. Learn the spirityal approach to dealing with anxiety and depression, as well as what to say and how to cope in such situations. Appreciate the use of prayers in these times. The benefits you will receive from all of this will be beyond measure for yourself and for your spouse.

7) Whether you are in school or working, you may have the practical need to take some time off. A professor or dean will generally be more understanding if you give him an honest explanation early on, instead of attempting to avoid the "stigma" by not explaining anything, but still constantly showing up late to classes. For those in the work force, be aware of the FMLA (Family and Medical Leave Act). This may entitle you to take off up to twelve weeks of work (unpaid) without losing your job or any accompanying benefits. Alternatively, now may be the best time to use a block of sick days and/or unpaid vacation days. Students might consider taking a semester off or taking an academic leave of absence. Any of these steps can be of enormous benefit to your wife's—and your own—peace of mind.

Our society puts great pressure on new mothers to resume work quickly themselves, to jump back into the stress and responsibility of their jobs. For some, the work is an outlet and positive experience. However, for many, the job can be overwhelming and exhausting in the months after childbirth—even for a woman who does not have postpartum complications. If your wife has such a job, it is important to let her know that other options exist for her as well, and that you're ready to explore them as needed. This can be a source of tremendous relief and calmness for her.

One more thing: Above all, never confront your wife in front of your children, even if you are upset. Even younger children can be very perceptive in detecting nuances, such as facial expression and body language. You should explain to your children that right now their mommy is feeling tired and sad—but that in no way is this their fault. Stress that you're getting mommy all the extra help that she needs, and that you're sure, with G-d's help, that she'll be feeling better soon.

You remain the most important person to your wife's continued functioning and eventual recovery, but do not succumb to the pressures of stigma and a misplaced sense of independence.

We all must rely on the Divine assistance, as well as on the kindness and support of other people at such times. Hopefully, this test will only serve to strengthen your relationship with your spouse, and will also further your own character development and inner strength as a caring and productive individual.

Ask the Professional

The following "Ask the Professional" section is intended for educational purposes only. Neither the publisher nor any of their employees, the author, or any of the physicians listed in this book assume any liability for any of the information presented herein. Always consult a competent health care professional before making any medically-related decision.

Ask the Psychologist

Dr. Mara Tesler Stein, Psy.D
Chicago, IL

Clinical Psychologist, specializing in fertility, pregnancy and postpartum stress

What are some of the early warning signs of PPD?

For many women, the earliest symptom is a strong feeling of unease with no definitive cause. A new mother might feel restless or more unfocused than she would have expected even with a new baby and could have difficulty shaking this off with normal activity. Some women describe feeling "off" and sense that something is amiss, without being able to pinpoint exactly what is wrong. The new mother may say to herself, "I'm not myself; this is not me."

For some women, this sense of uneasiness progresses into more debilitating feelings of sadness, anxiety, or confusion. Some begin to experience panic attacks, obsessive thought patterns (many times regarding the baby's health), and/or excessive guilt. A woman may also lose interest in her usual activities.

As the illness intensifies, physical symptoms, such as headaches, numbness, tingling in limbs, chest pains, heart palpitations, and hyperventilation, can occur. Significant changes in eating and sleeping patterns will usually present themselves; a hallmark of PPD is being unable to sleep even when the baby sleeps, as well as a pervasive sense of despair and hopelessness.

A woman suffering from PPD will often blame herself for not being "happy", and might worry that she is undeserving of her child. She may feel guilty that she is not the mother that she had envisioned herself to be. These deprecating thought patterns typically make the symptoms of anxiety and depression worse.

༄༅

Which women are at significant risk?

Although PPD can technically happen to any woman who has just given birth, there are some individuals who are statisti-

cally at a higher risk. These women would include those who:
  *have just given birth to their first child
  *have experienced a high-risk pregnancy, traumatic delivery, or a pre-term birth
  *have experienced a previous pregnancy-related loss (e.g., miscarriage or stillbirth)
  *have a personal or family history of mood and/or anxiety disorders
  *have experienced a previous episode of PPD
  *are lacking marital harmony
  *are lacking financial stability
  *are lacking a social network of family and friends
  *have just made an unexpected or recent move

ಬಿ ಛ

What is the difference between a psychologist, psychiatrist, psychotherapist, and social worker? How does one determine from which professional to seek help?

A psychologist has completed a doctoral level of clinical training and will usually have a title of Ph.D or Psy.D. A psychiatrist is a medical doctor, an M.D., who has completed 4 years of medical school and a residency in psychiatry. Psychiatrists are able to prescribe medication and often work together with a psychologist.

A social worker has an L.C.S.W. or M.S.W. (with a master's degree in clinical social work). A psychotherapist is a generic title that is more descriptive of the activity of psychotherapy than the background, training, or orientation of the person offering the therapeutic service. For those who specialize in psychotherapy, which is a form of talk therapy, psychologists, psychiatrists, and social workers can all use this descriptive title to let people know what services they offer. Psychotherapists without any other title or degree to back up their training and experience should be researched carefully, as without more information about the person's background, the title means little and can be used without discretion.

One who is suffering from PPD should make sure to utilize a professional who is specifically trained and skilled to address **women's mental health issues**. This is vital to know when making inquires, as some mental health professionals have only superficial training in this area, while others have gone through extensive training programs and fellowships that specifically focus on women's mental health.

Which type of professional to seek guidance from is a personal choice, although I would recommend someone who has established collaborative relationships with women's health psychiatrists, in the event that medication is necessary. One should always make sure to seek help from a professional who has a solid name and reputation in the community. One should also be careful to choose someone who is a "good fit" for her own personal style. Information about different professionals can be obtained through referral services, and most effectively by word of mouth. Women should feel free to call therapists to inquire about their therapy approach and to get a sense of "fit" from the initial contact.

ೞ ೞ

What are some of the techniques a therapist might use in treatment? What role does medication play?

Each treatment is individualized and tailor-made for the client at hand. However, all skilled therapists will begin by taking a history in order to better understand the context within which the current symptoms arise. Especially when the woman (and her family) are suffering, therapists will attempt to offer some initial pragmatic solutions for how to deal with the "here and now", meaning the emotional distress that is affecting the client presently and disrupting her daily routine. For instance, if a woman is experiencing severe anxiety, initial treatment may include learning about panic and anxiety and practicing techniques that can help prevent or manage panic attacks. Some examples of this include progressive muscle relaxation, as well as cognitive techniques to address distortions or intrusive thoughts. This method of treatment is referred to as CBT, or cognitive behavioral therapy.

While some symptoms can be addressed and alleviated by talk therapy alone, other symptoms, such as intrusive thoughts that can come with certain types of anxiety, may have a strong organic component and can often be helped rapidly and effectively with the use of medication. Severe depressive symptoms which hinder a woman's ability to interact appropriately with her child, as well as disrupt her daily routine, will also require medication. Depending on the types of medications used, some may provide immediate relief and others may take some weeks to begin to take effect.

After the "here and now" is under control, therapists and clients will often begin to examine the history and context that may have contributed to or escalated the PPD episode.

For example, clients who are perfectionists in nature or unrealistic in their expectations, can address the ways in which their thinking patterns set them up for anxiety or disappointment. Those who tend to never express their fears and feelings can learn how to do this in healthy ways.

Once these underlying issues are processed, with the help of the therapist, the client is relieved of a tremendous sense of inner pressure that she had been placing on herself, with healing occurring along the way. This method of treatment is known as "inside-oriented psychotherapy". Many experienced therapists utilize a combination of psychotherapy techniques, integrating the relationship building and depth orientation of inside-oriented therapy with the concrete techniques of cognitive-behavioral therapies.

When medication is recommended, it is used to help the woman sleep, eat, and think more clearly, so that the treatments mentioned above can be more effective. Research has shown that those individuals treated with medication alone have a very high rate of relapse, as they have not been given solid tools to deal with emotional distress in the future. It is therefore highly recommended that a woman taking medication seek some form of therapy as well.

ೞ ೃ

Is the ratio of PPD victims higher in our community than in the general population? Why or why not?

I am not aware of any clinical studies that have been done to measure the ratio of PPD between the Orthodox Jewish community and the general population.

I would surmise, though, that PPD is a relatively common problem in our community. We tend to have large families, and as families spread out and become more isolated from families of origin, they are often lacking the extended family support system that used to be common. Having many children **does not cause** PPD to occur, but it will, even in the best circumstances, raise the level of stress in a household. As I've mentioned before, high levels of stress can be a trigger for PPD.

ೞ ೃ

What role does a woman's support system play in treatment?

The relationship between a woman's support system and level of PPD is significant. In fact, we only need to look at the prevalence of PPD and related emotional disorders in the last few decades to see that it has increased in number, as families became more nuclear, and women were left vulnerable during this transitional period after childbirth.

It is also clear to see that women who are more socially isolated due to specific circumstances (e.g. they live geographically far from others, are stay-at-home moms who don't get out a lot, etc.) tend to suffer from PPD more than their peers who are not as isolated. Therefore, social contact and peer support during the very real adjustments and stresses of new parenthood is an important strategy for preventing and addressing PPD.

The husband's role cannot be dismissed. Marital support should be strengthened by defining shared responsibilities and implementing realistic coping methods during the postpartum adjustment period.

It would also be wise for new mothers to confer with family and supportive friends about their concerns related to childrearing. Many times, new mothers fear that their concerns reflect badly on themselves as mothers. Voicing these fears can help them to see how common most feelings and worries are after a new baby is born.

Another important aspect is to arrange for babysitting and household help in order to leave quality "down" time for the new parents to rest and have time for each other. I would also strongly recommend that new mothers make every effort to get out of the house **daily** and interact with others, even at a superficial level. This can help one to feel less disconnected and less isolated, even before the desire to be out and about returns.

How long is a typical therapy session and how many are needed over the course of treatment?

A typical session lasts for about one hour. How many are needed depends on each individual and everyone's unique circumstances.

༄༅

How much does a session cost? Does health insurance cover the cost of mental health treatment? Are there community resources/sliding scales available for those who can't afford the full price? If so, how does one go about obtaining financial aid?

A typical session will cost about $100-$160 for a professional trained at a doctoral level, and about $75-$100 for others. There are some professionals who will charge a much higher rate and those who will offer a sliding scale for those who cannot afford their fees.

Many therapists will accept major insurances carriers, but the rate of reimbursement and type of coverage varies greatly depending on one's contract with his or her insurance company. For providers within one's insurance network, coverage can be as high as 90% of the fee. For those out of network, insurance will often cover between 50% and 80%. Legislation has recently passed in the United States that requires insurance companies to cover mental health treatments under the same conditions as medical treatments. This means that insurance companies can no longer impose different standards and limits on mental health coverage than the limits they set on other medical coverage. Be sure to ask your therapist about this if you have questions.

Since it is important to find a mental health professional whom the family can afford, and who is culturally sensitive to the needs of the Jewish community, I would recommend speaking to a rabbi or community leader for guidance. They will hopefully know about any clinical services that are offered through the community and will usually know about community services that can loan money or help to defray costs. If you are comfortable sharing your experience with close friends or family members, you might be surprised to discover that they have some experience with psychotherapy and can make some recommendations. Many times, calling one therapist and asking advice regarding a more specialized referral can help you get to someone who is the right fit for you.

ಲ ಡ

Do you see the family (e.g. husband, parents, or older children) as a unit during treatment, or do you just focus on the afflicted mother?

It is a good idea for both new parents to come to a few sessions in order to discuss the family's adjustment to the new baby and the specific symptoms that are of concern. A husband can learn more about what his wife is experiencing and gain more understanding about the importance of his support and collaboration in her recovery. It is also a good opportunity for the husband to voice concerns or ask any questions that he may have.

If one's husband cannot, or will not, participate in therapy sessions, a woman can still reap the benefits of treatment. Many times, a therapist will encourage the mother to bring her baby, especially if the mother has expressed worries about attachment or separation. It is not common for other members of the extended family to participate in treatment, unless there is a specific reason to do so.

What message would you give to someone reading this book who thinks that she may be suffering from PPD?

PPD is a documented illness that has been described for centuries. You are not making this up; it is **not** "all in your mind"—despite your own worries or what others may tell you. By reaching out for help, not only will you help yourself heal, but in the process, you will gain valuable self-help skills that will last you for a lifetime. Additionally, by getting help, you are also helping your baby develop cognitively and emotionally. Depression and anxiety in mothers have a documented impact on their growing children. Help yourself and your family by reaching out for help.

Ask the Psychiatrist

Dr. Laura J. Miller, MD
Boston, MA

Former Director of UIC Women's Mental Health Program, Author of Postpartum Mood Disorders (American Psychiatric, 1999)
Brigham and Women's Hospital—A Teaching Affiliate of Harvard Medical School

What is the physiological cause of PPD?

During pregnancy, a woman's level of estrogen, progesterone, and prolactin, three important hormones in the endocrine system, are steadily rising. These hormones directly affect the level of neurotransmitters, whose purpose is to serve as the connecting links between brain cells and facilitate optimal brain functioning.

Estrogen will boost a neurotransmitter named serotonin, which stabilizes mood; progesterone will boost a neurotransmitter named GABA (gamma amino butyric acid), whose function is to keep anxiety in check; and prolactin is used to help prepare the mother's body for milk production.

In response to these elevated hormonal levels, the brain will automatically reduce the number of receptors on each cell to keep the activity of the "supercharged" neurotransmitters at a healthy level. Without the extra receptors, the increased amounts of serotonin and GABA cannot attach themselves to the cells and "overload" the brain. In essence, during pregnancy, we have a natural safety latch in place to help keep neurotransmitters in proper balance.

Immediately after giving birth, estrogen and progesterone levels will begin to drop rapidly back to pre-pregnancy levels, while prolactin will remain elevated to help build and maintain an adequate milk supply. The sharp decrease of estrogen and progesterone will subsequently lead to a lowered level of serotonin and GABA. At the same time, the brain will also begin to build its base of receptors back up to its pre-pregnancy state.

Postpartum depression and/or anxiety will occur, from a physiological standpoint, when the neurotransmitters serotonin and GABA remain **too** low and/or if the brain has not built up its receptors base **fast enough**. Both of these factors can drastically impact on the mood and/or anxiety level of a woman who is biologically susceptible, as her hormonal system is essentially off-kilter and directly affecting her brain functioning. In general, if a woman will experience a PPD reaction stemming specifically from this source, it will occur in the first six to eight weeks after giving birth.

The other postulated cause of PPD is based on the woman's stress response, and can be triggered for up to a full year after the birth. The physiologic system that responds to environmental stress, known as the "HPA axis", is more sensitive and vulnerable as a result of childbirth. In other words, a woman will feel stressed out **faster** than usual, and her feelings will be of a more **intense** nature. If one's stress levels are too high during this postpartum period when the stress system is already very vulnerable, actual changes in brain chemistry can take place leading to lowered levels of serotonin and GABA. This alteration in brain chemistry can easily lead to PPD symptoms.

ಬಿ ಬ

What is the clinical difference between Baby Blues, Postpartum Depression, and Postpartum Psychosis?

Baby Blues

This is a very common reaction after childbirth and affects at least 50% of new mothers. It is hypothesized to be a result of an elevated level of a hormone named oxytocin, which is related to milk production. The symptoms begin three to five days after childbirth, when the mother's milk supply comes in and oxytocin is at its peak.

The role of oxytocin is an important one. It helps promote feelings of bonding and attachment between mother and child. The strong emotions that come along with this process will be generalized, and the new mom will feel intense about **everything**—both in a positive and negative manner. This explains the mood swings that a woman may experience after birth, where she may feel exhilarated one moment, only to find herself teary-eyed the next. Baby Blues will usually last about two to four weeks in most women.

Postpartum Depression

When a woman's predominant feeling is sad, empty, or apathetic, and this lasts for most of her day for a number of weeks, she may be suffering from Postpartum Depression. This serious reaction will affect up to 20% of new mothers. The afflicted woman often has significant changes in her eating and sleeping patterns (eating and sleeping either more or less than usual). Intense anxiety and problems with concentration may present themselves along with the depressive symptoms.

Post Partum Psychosis

This is a less common postpartum reaction that will affect approximately 1 out of every 1000 new mothers. It is more prevalent among women who suffer from Bipolar Disorder, yet it can happen to those without this condition as well. Postpartum Psychosis will almost always manifest itself within the first four weeks after delivery. A woman suffering from this condition may experience all the usual PPD symptoms, as well as symptoms which are psychotic in nature. Examples of psychotic symptoms would include hallucinations, where one sees, hears, or feels something that is not really there, or delusions, where a woman may harbor beliefs which are not factual in nature.

‍ ‍

What role do anxiety disorders play in PPD?

Although Postpartum Depression is discussed more often, Postpartum Anxiety Disorders are common as well.

A woman experiencing anxiety after childbirth may suffer from Postpartum Panic Disorder, Postpartum Obsessive Compulsive Disorder (OCD) or Postpartum Post-Traumatic Stress Disorder (PTSD).

PTSD in particular may be linked to an extremely traumatic labor or delivery, a premature or sickly newborn, or a previously experienced, pregnancy-related loss. Panic and OCD symptoms are very physiological in nature and usually manifest themselves during pregnancy or in the first six to eight weeks after the birth. PTSD usually begins early on, but is often not diagnosed right away.

In general, although Postpartum Depression and Postpartum Anxiety are two separate types of disorders, one often leads to the other. For example, if a woman is anxiety-ridden and cannot sleep, her daily functioning will be affected and this may lead her to feel overwhelmed and depressed. Conversely, if a woman is depressed, she may begin to feel anxious about how her baby is being affected as a result. Clinicians will usually label the depression and anxiety as either primary or secondary based on which symptoms appeared first, (e.g. primary depression, secondary anxiety) and treat the woman accordingly.

ಐ ಬ

How common is PPD in the general population? In the Orthodox Jewish Population?

PPD is estimated to affect between 10-20% of new mothers. As far as specific figures for the Orthodox community—I don't think that there were any epidemiological studies done to assess that. I will tell you, however, that as a psychiatrist affiliated with a major hospital, I have seen firsthand how PPD affects women from **all** cultures and backgrounds. Orthodox Jewish women are no exception to this rule. I have treated many women from the

Orthodox Jewish community who mistakenly assume that they are the only one experiencing this common illness.

There are studies which show that within certain groups where social support is incredibly strong and organized (e.g. African tribal communities), the rates of PPD may be lower. This is in stark contrast to the more westernized world where, in general, there is a lack of proper social support offered to a new mother.

ಲ ಌ

Is PPD a genetic disorder?

As I've mentioned before, PPD is physiological in nature for many woman and may therefore have a genetic component. This does **not** mean that one whose relative experienced PPD is destined to experience PPD as well; as every person's individual biological make-up is different. In addition, one will never know for certain if a family member's PPD was triggered by environmental factors as opposed to physiological factors.

Nevertheless, one should take note if one's first-degree relative (e.g. mother or sister) experienced PPD, and perhaps discuss this with one's OB-GYN or primary care doctor before or during pregnancy.

ಲ ಌ

What is the role of a psychiatrist in treatment? A psychologist? A holistic healer? How does one determine which course of treatment to follow?

The first thing a woman should do when she experiences a PPD reaction is to schedule a thorough diagnostic evaluation. This can be administered by select primary doctors or

OB-GYNs who are specifically trained, or, more commonly, by a psychiatrist who specializes in women's mental health. This thorough evaluation is specifically designed to assess current symptoms and key factors that have led up to the present PPD episode.

Based on the results of the evaluation, a diagnosis will be made (e.g. Postpartum Depression, Postpartum Psychosis, Postpartum PTSD, Postpartum OCD, Postpartum Panic Disorder, etc.). A detailed plan of treatment will then be laid out.

In general, primary treatment would consist of a psychiatrist who would administer medication if necessary, and a psychologist or social worker who would address psychotherapy. (In some cases, psychiatrists are trained to do both.) Adjunctive treatment would deal with nutritional counseling, exercise regiments, acupuncture, etc. and would be implemented under the guidance of a knowledgeable physician, nutritionist, or holistic healer.

ೞ ಣ

Which medications would a psychiatrist typically recommend for a woman suffering from depressive symptoms, anxious symptoms, insomnia, or psychosis?

A psychiatrist will choose a medication for a patient based on its effectiveness, side effects, and cost. If a mother is breastfeeding her baby, this will be taken into account as well. A psychiatrist will be careful to choose either an "activating" drug or a "calming" drug based on the type of PPD response that is being experienced by the patient.

The most common classes of medications used to treat PPD and related disorders are listed below:

Selective Serotonin Reuptake Inhibitors (SSRI's)
Selective Noraepinephrine Reuptake Inhibitors (SNRI's)

Mono Amine Oxidase Inhibitors (MAOI's)
Tricyclides
For Postpartum Psychosis and insomnia, other medications would be commonly prescribed.

☙ ☜

What is the success rate for treating PPD with medication?

If one treats PPD with medication alone, there is a 65-70% recovery rate on average. If one treats PPD with medication in conjunction with psychotherapy and other measures, the success rate is close to 100%.

It is important to note that if one treats the PPD with medication alone, there is a significant chance of relapse once the medicine is stopped. This is especially true if there are ongoing risk factors in the woman's environment. Psychotherapy focuses on preventive care, where the client is taught techniques to empower herself during times of stress, which, as discussed before, are key triggers of PPD and related disorders.

☙ ☜

What are the most common side effects from the medications discussed above? What are the percentages of these occurrences?

Answer:
In general, the most commonly reported side effects are:
-headaches
-nausea
-dizziness

-weight loss or weight gain
-increased restlessness or fatigue
-physical changes in the area of marital intimacy
-weakened bone structure (can be counteracted by calcium and vitamin D supplements)

Most people will experience some side effects when beginning to take medication, but usually these side effects will diminish in frequency and intensity, or even disappear, within the first few weeks. For some very sensitive individuals, side effects may linger or be especially troublesome. If this is the case, the doctor should be consulted.

Sometimes, a doctor will recommend starting at a very low dose and building up gradually to a full dose, so that the body can get used to the new medication.

ಶಿ ಲ

Should one discontinue treatment if side effects are severe? Is there any solution to this problem?

One should never stop taking medication abruptly, as severe and sometimes dangerous withdrawal symptoms may occur. Rather, a woman should always consult with her doctor if she feels that the medication is not helping and/or is causing serious side effects.

We are fortunate to have many medications to choose from in our day; one must keep trying until she finds one that is effective for her specific body chemistry. A woman who is sensitive to medication in general can take a special blood test, which will show how she metabolizes different classes of drugs. A doctor can evaluate the results and subsequently prescribe an appropriate medication that would more likely be effective.

ಶಿ ಲ

What is the risk of not treating PPD? Will it go away on its own? How long could that take?

PPD will usually linger for a minimum of six months if left untreated. It frequently will last many more months and sometimes even years. For a minority of women, the PPD reaction may fade somewhat, yet remain as a chronic illness.

The risk of not treating PPD can be significant, as it can affect future episodes of the illness. A woman who experiences PPD after a subsequent childbirth may experience more acute and longer-lasting symptoms. The condition may also be harder to treat. This psychological phenomenon, known as "kindling", occurs when brain chemistry falls back into a previously experienced pattern and becomes more entrenched in nature.

In contrast, one whose PPD was addressed the first time around, before the brain chemistry is altered significantly, will not be subject to this reaction.

෨෬

Can PPD repeat itself in future pregnancies? Can one do anything to avoid it?

One who has experienced a PPD reaction once will always remain at a higher risk than other women for future episodes.

It would be prudent for a woman who has experienced PPD in the past to see a women's mental health psychiatrist before a new pregnancy, for pre-conceptive counseling. This is the current preventative manner used to address PPD in high-risk women. It involves an analysis of the woman's history and current environmental circumstances. Based on the assessment, the mental health professional will set up a preventative treatment plan, which may include any combination of the following: nutritional counseling, vitamin supplements, prophylactic medication, stress management techniques, aerobic exercise routine, etc.

ಬಿಲ್

Are there psychiatrists trained to treat PPD as their specialty?

Yes. They are called "women's mental health psychiatrists" and/or "reproductive psychiatrists". These mental health professionals have received extensive training in treating PPD and related disorders.

Although they are a minority in number, these specially trained mental health professionals are steadily increasing as awareness grows and more grants are awarded for training and research.

If one would like to find a women's health psychiatrist in her city, she can contact an organization known as "NASPOG", which stands for "North American Society for Psychosocial Obstetrics and Gynecology". This group does not directly provide referrals, but can tell you who their members are in a given area.

ಬಿಲ್

Do insurance companies recognize PPD as a condition and cover costs?

It is best to check with the insurance company, since policies differ. Private insurances often cover PPD-related services under their mental health benefits.

If a woman finds herself suffering from a PPD reaction and does not have any insurance coverage or means of payment, help can still be found. She should go to her local community mental health clinic for assistance. As such clinics are city funded or privately funded (through grants), they usually offer services free of charge or on a sliding scale for those who qualify.

❧☙

What is the current medical attitude towards PPD? How has this changed over the last generation? What is the general community's attitude to it? The Orthodox Jewish community's attitude?

In 1994, PPD was added to the DSM-IV, which is the definitive diagnostic manual used to label and classify mental health disorders. As a result, PPD became more publicized and studied in depth by experts across the country. We are definitely heading in the right direction, although stigma and misconceptions associated with PPD still remain a problem for many.

There are presently mental health professionals who train primary care doctors, obstetricians, and pediatricians how to spot and help a new mother with PPD. Our program alone has trained over 5,000 doctors.

As far as the attitude of the Orthodox Jewish community, I am seeing that more of their members are reaching out for help as public awareness grows. Yet, just as in the general population, there is still a large element of misunderstanding and confusion about the illness. As a result, the stigma attached to PPD remains strong.

❧☙

What message would you give to someone reading this book who thinks that she may be suffering from PPD?

I have specialized in this field for many years and have treated many strong, courageous, and spiritually devout individuals who are phenomenally successful in their personal lives, and yet were still afflicted by this painful disorder. PPD can happen to anyone, and it is **not** a reflection on you as a person or parent.

Reach out for the help you need if you are suffering. With the proper treatment and support, you can and will recover.

Ask the Nurse Practitioner

Rebecca Christophersen, APN, CNP
Boston, MA

Women's Mental Health Nurse Practitioner
Incorporating the Holistic/Nutritional Approach in Treating PPD

What is the relationship between nutrition and pregnancy/postpartum recovery?

There is definitely a correlation between a nutritious diet and a healthy pregnancy and postpartum period. When a woman is pregnant, additional stress is placed upon her body. Metabolism speeds up, fluid and blood flow increase, and significant hormonal changes take place. All of this occurs in order to help create a protective environment for the developing fetus.

An expectant woman should make every effort to help fortify and strengthen this environment for her child. This can be accomplished by living a healthy lifestyle, which would include taking care to eat a well-rounded and healthy diet. Daily diets should include at least five fruits and vegetables a day, lean protein, and whole grains. Foods which contain calcium, iron, zinc, selenium, iodine, vitamins C and D, folate, omega-3 essential fatty acids, and B complex will help keep mother and child in top form.

In particular, fetal brain development is especially sensitive to the maternal diet. If the mother is lacking important nutrients, especially omega-3 essential fatty acids (specifically DHA), neural connections and cellular growth may be impeded. A fetus may also develop spina bifida if there is a deficiency of folate in the diet.

It would be prudent for a woman to begin building up the proper nutrients in her system **before** her pregnancy begins—ideally one year before, and at the very least, three months before. One can schedule a pre-conceptive visit with a health care provider to discuss a proper food and diet plan. Pre-planning is the key to creating a healthy, nutrient-complete pregnancy.

After the birth, the new mother should continue to eat well and try to live a healthy lifestyle. By doing so, she will help build and maintain an adequate milk supply, as well as keep her physical and emotional health in check. There are studies which indicate a link between vitamin deficiency and Postpartum Depression. It would be best to try to avoid this emotional upheaval by continuing to adhere to a nutritious and balanced diet.

☙ ☬

What effects will a mother's nutritional choices have on a breast-fed baby?

A woman who chooses to breastfeed her child needs to be aware that everything she eats or drinks will be broken down and passed along to her baby. She needs to be as conscientious and mindful of her food choices as she was during pregnancy

If a mother is taking care to eat a balanced diet consistently, she is probably getting the nutrients that she needs. However, I would still recommend that she take a quality multivitamin (or continue her prenatal vitamin) as a precaution. Although medical literature is mixed on the necessity of supplements due to a lack of evidence-based information, clinical studies indicate that many women do benefit from them.

☙ ☬

What would constitute a healthy diet for a new mom? Any specific foods to focus on? Anything to avoid?

A healthy, well-balanced diet includes a variety of foods from all food groups. An emphasis should be placed on:

Whole grain items versus those made with refined white flour

Foods containing **iron** (such as red meat, chicken, beans, and eggs)

Foods containing **folic acid** (such as green leafy vegetables and whole grains)

Vitamin C (found in citrus fruits and juices)

Vitamin D (can be absorbed into the body through sunlight and by drinking fortified milk)

Omega-3 essential fatty acids (found in freshwater fish such as salmon, whitefish, and tuna*, avocado, nuts, and fortified soy milk)

Calcium (found in dairy products, spinach, and fortified soy milk)

8-10 glasses of **water** a day to keep the body well-hydrated and to help flush out one's system

All foods are allowed in moderation on a balanced diet. Lactating women should avoid alcoholic beverages.

*to be eaten in limited quantities due to high levels of mercury

༄༅༄༅

Omegas 3, 6, and 9 are constantly being proclaimed as super-foods that enhance one's mood. What is your opinion on this?

There is legitimacy to this claim. Omega-3, 6, and 9, which are all variations of the same source (essential fatty acids/DHA), help promote and maintain good brain connections and cellular growth. They also ensure that neurotransmitters are connecting properly, which leads to emotional equilibrium and wellbeing.

༄༅༄༅

Many women are advised to take medication to treat PPD. Can one substitute nutritional supplements in-

stead? Are there any other holistic remedies that are successful?

This depends on the individual woman and the severity of her symptoms. Is she functioning in daily life? Is she bonding properly with her baby? How is her interaction with her spouse and other family members? These are the questions one must ask. The whole picture must be taken into account in order to make an informed decision.

Medications used to treat PPD are designed to address and treat specific areas of the brain, whereas proper nutrition and vitamin supplements help in a more generalized manner, promoting positive activity throughout the whole area.

Many women whom I see are strongly opposed to taking medication, but with increased knowledge and public awareness, this route is clearly becoming more socially acceptable. Mothers are starting to realize that a woman suffering from PPD, whose system is essentially in a prolonged state of the "fight or flight" mode, is putting herself and her baby at risk. When women realize that their babies may be adversely affected, they are usually more receptive to the idea of taking medication to treat PPD. The goal is to eliminate symptoms of PPD, and to create a more balanced environment for the pregnancy and postpartum period.

Regardless of the need for prescribed medication to treat PPD, I always recommend a vitamin regimen. This may or may not be helpful to a woman suffering from severe PPD, as the vitamins need time to build up in the body. If a woman's functioning is impaired by her PPD, she may need help faster. However, a vitamin regimen may be the appropriate choice for someone suffering from mild symptoms. In general, I find that a vitamin regimen works best as a **preventative** measure, to be used before serious symptoms appear. The vitamins are also useful in **maintaining** emotional equilibrium.

Holistic remedies such as massage, yoga, and acupuncture may work well for a woman who is experiencing mild symptoms, or as an adjunct to medication and therapy for those experiencing severe PPD. I find that any activity that a woman perceives as fun and positive helps her to focus exclusively on **herself** for a designated amount of time, which will help promote healing and rejuvenation.

༄༅

A thyroid problem can easily mimic PPD symptoms. What can be done from a nutritional standpoint to regulate this problem?

During pregnancy, thyroid function slows down, whereas soon after delivery it speeds up again. This fluctuation can throw the body off-kilter and lead the thyroid to overproduce (hyperthyroidism) after giving birth. For some women, the problem actually begins in pregnancy if thyroid function is too suppressed (hypothyroidism).

Although there is not much medical data available on this, it is believed that an adequate amount of iodine can help prevent the imbalance. Pregnant women should take care not to totally eliminate salty foods from their diet (although they should not be adding any extra salt either).

Thyroid dysfunction can lead a woman to feel depressed and lethargic, or anxious and jumpy. Women should request a blood test from their health care provider to rule out a thyroid problem if they have not yet been tested for it. If an imbalance is noted, usually a drug named Synthroid or a similar agent will be prescribed to help correct the imbalance.

Many new mothers are eager to shed the extra weight that they gained in pregnancy. Would you recommend diet foods and/or artificial sweeteners?

Any diet fad should be avoided. Diets in general only serve to provide acute "quick fixes". The weight is almost always gained back. A balanced food plan in conjunction with mild to moderate exercise is the key to permanent weight loss and maintenance.

I personally don't think diet food is any less safe than an abundance of sugar. Both diet soda and regular soda are okay in moderate amounts, when incorporated into a well-balanced, healthy diet. However, when consumed in excess, both are detrimental to mother and baby. The operative word is *moderation.*

☼☾

Are there any specific foods and/or nutritional supplements to help a new mother who is having trouble with low milk supply, sleeping or concentrating?

A well-balanced diet, regular exercise, and a good multivitamin may help prevent these difficulties. Taking time to relax, as well as sleeping when the baby does, are also important measures for a new mother to take.

There are some herbal remedies available which are used to help increase milk supply. As most are not monitored under government-controlled agencies (e.g. Food and Drug Administration), they should be evaluated by one's pediatrician before use. Melatonin supplements can be used to help regulate sleep patterns, and foods rich in omega-3 essential fatty acids will help to enhance concentration.

What message would you give to someone reading this book who thinks that she may be suffering from PPD?

Don't let societal pressures decide what is "right". Do what you need to do in order to function at your best. If necessary, lower your standards and expectations related to child-rearing and recognize that your abilities are unique to you. It is therefore counterproductive to compare yourself to your peers. The barometer of success should be based on effort and not outcome. Feel good knowing that by trying your hardest, you are reaching **your** potential.

Every new mother should take care to recognize that a suffering mother leads to a suffering baby, whether this is obvious or not. Your baby's brain development and social attachment style, both of which will have great impact on his future, depend on you and the choices you are making for yourself today. Take good care of yourself and seek outside help if necessary, so that your child will thrive and one day thank you for it!

Ask the OB-GYN

Dr. Barbara S. Robinson, MD
Kenosha, WI

OB-GYN, Midwest Center Women's Health

Are obstetricians trained to spot and treat PPD, or is this the job of a mental health professional?

Obstetricians are usually the first line of help for mothers suffering from PPD; as such, we are trained to both spot and treat the disorder. In fact, one of the primary purposes of the six-week postpartum check-up is to assess the woman's emotional state.

During this visit, I will ask the new mom pertinent questions such as: How are you coping? How much sleep are you getting? Are you eating well?

Based on the responses I receive, I am usually able to get a good sense of how the mom is doing. Other physicians may not feel as comfortable with this direct approach and may present the mother with a prepared questionnaire, where answers are rated in order to identify a patient who is at risk for PPD.

Once PPD is suspected, an OB-GYN will often refer the new mother to a counselor or a psychologist for treatment and further monitoring. If medication is deemed necessary, an OB-GYN can prescribe it, although many feel more comfortable having a psychiatrist do so. This is especially true if the mother's symptoms seem severe or non-conventional in nature.

If a woman begins to experience PPD symptoms a *few months* after childbirth, should she still be contacting her obstetrician?

Absolutely. PPD is an illness which, by definition, can occur any time during the first year after childbirth. A woman should not hesitate to call her OB-GYN during this time if she has any concerns. It is the responsibility of all OB-GYNs to help their patients, whether it is a few weeks or a few months after delivery.

Obstetricians also recognize that many women of childbearing age do not have frequent access to other doctors. Many may be seeing only their OB-GYN and their child's pediatrician during the first year after childbirth. It is therefore important to keep the lines of communication open and encourage patients to reach out to their doctor for guidance.

ಐಞ

Are your patients comfortable confiding in you about their PPD? Do they appear open about their symptoms? Ashamed? What is your general reaction to their disclosure?

I actually find that many women who are experiencing PPD do not even realize it initially. Sure, most people have vaguely heard of the term "Postpartum Depression" but, as with all illnesses, they tend to think it only affects "other" individuals.

When I question my patients during the six-week postpartum check-up and we begin to talk, I find out about the lack of sleep, the loss of appetite, and the excessive crying. When I inform these woman that they may be suffering from PPD, they usually appear deeply ashamed. They express sentiments of feeling "defective" and "completely alone". I hear this from women of all ages and from all backgrounds.

My standard reaction to my patients is, "There is nothing to be ashamed of. You didn't do anything wrong; PPD can happen to anyone." If they resist treatment, I will use an analogy to explain how I view this illness, comparing it to a case of pneumonia. Would one be embarrassed to go to a doctor and be prescribed antibiotics? Of course not, as the pneumonia is clearly not a reflection of the person. PPD, a condition caused by physiological changes in the body, is no different and should be regarded in a similar manner.

ঔ ৩

Is it important for new patients to inform you about a past PPD episode when discussing their medical history? Why or why not?

A women who has had a past PPD experience should be sure to let her doctor know about this as soon as possible, as statistically she is at a higher risk for recurrence. An OB-GYN can use this information to help patients in two ways:

*setting up a support system for the woman. The woman can be put in touch with a counselor or therapist as a preventative measure during her pregnancy. This way, if the need arises, she has those who can assist her.

*discussing possible medications that can be taken during pregnancy or immediately after the birth in order to help prevent another PPD episode.

ঔ ৩

Which PPD symptoms do you find are the most common?

The most common symptoms that I see are excessive crying and a general inability to cope. I also have a lot of women report to me that they just can't fall asleep, even when the house is quiet and the baby is napping. Many women will also experience a loss of appetite.

Other symptoms that I hear about, although less than the ones mentioned above, are linked to excessive anxiety. Women will tell me that they worry about what kind of mother they are. Nothing that they do as a parent seems "good enough". They will say things like, "I'm going to fail as a mother; I'm going to let my baby down…" Some women will also experience full-blown panic attacks.

In your experience, have you seen a correlation between PPD and high-risk pregnancy, pre-term delivery, and/or C-section?

I do see a correlation between a traumatic pregnancy/delivery and how a woman copes afterward. However, I find that these women, who generally had high expectations about their pregnancy/delivery that were not met, usually have a hard time during the immediate **"baby blues"** stage which occurs in the first few weeks postpartum. They may experience the "blues" for a longer amount of time and perhaps in a more intense manner than their peers who did not have such traumatic pregnancies/deliveries. However, most will not be afflicted by true PPD. The ones who will experience PPD probably had a physiological susceptibility, which may have been triggered by the upsetting event. It is important to remember that PPD can affect anyone, regardless of the events leading up to or during delivery.

As an obstetrician who has much experience in the Orthodox Jewish community, how would you rate our reaction and attitude towards PPD? Does this differ from your other patients?

I find that almost all my patients who experience PPD react with intense shame, **regardless of their cultural background**. Society as a whole seems to have a "not in my backyard" approach towards mental health issues. I do not think Orthodox Jews are unique in this regard.

❧

Do you find that a specific personality type seems to suffer from PPD more than others?

I have seen that PPD happens to all kinds of patients with all kinds of personalities. This just highlights my point that PPD is nothing to be ashamed of. You cannot **cause** it by having a certain kind of personality. If one is genetically inclined to PPD, she may be afflicted regardless of her personality.

❧

What message would you give to someone reading this book who thinks that she may be suffering from PPD?

Recognize that you are not alone, and that help is available. You need to seek this help for your baby's sake, and—although many mothers forget this—for your own sake, as well. Realize that your OB-GYN is there to help you with both the physical and psychological symptoms related to childbirth. Do not hesitate to contact us for guidance. We are here for you!

❧

Do you have any suggestions for how to help promote awareness and prevention of PPD in our community?

The key words are "education" and "awareness". Lectures, seminars, and articles directed to the average woman in our community will help her learn about what PPD really is and which symptoms warrant medical attention. Women should also be given clear guidelines of whom to contact for help/referrals.

Rabbis, doulas, OB-GYNs, mental health professionals, pediatricians and community leaders in general should network as much as possible. In this manner, referrals and treatment for those in need will be more efficient and respectful in nature.

Ask the Pediatrician

Dr. Steven B. Goldberg, MD, FAAP
Skokie, IL

Northshore University Healthcare System

What role does a mother's emotional state play in a baby's development during the first two years of life? Can any actions be done to prevent or negate possible damage to the baby caused by a new mother suffering from PPD?

The first two years of life are a time of critical development for a child. The baby's brain is newly formed; growing and developing at an outstanding rate. Crucial cognitive, motor, language, and social skills are being mastered and incorporated into daily life. If a mother who is suffering from Postpartum Depression is tense, unfocused, and apathetic to her baby, her child's development may be hindered.

A mother's primary role during these early years is to bond with her baby and be an effective nurturer. To accomplish this successfully, it is essential for the mother to be in a calm and focused state of mind, especially during feeding time, as this is an optimal time for bonding. The baby will also naturally acquire the skills mentioned above through this positive interaction. If a mother is suffering from serious PPD, other close family members (e.g. spouse, grandparents, etc.) should temporarily take over the role as effective nurturers. Quality time should be devoted to speaking and playing with the child until the mother is feeling better and can reassert her role as the primary caretaker.

If the child does not receive the cognitive, language, motor and social stimulation needed, serious delays may be noted, and developmental milestones may lag or be stymied. If this is the case, early intervention services may be instrumental in bridging the gap and helping the child catch up, but it **cannot** replace proper nurturing and bonding, which, as previously stated, is imperative during the first two years of life. Long-term effects may possibly be noted in this area. It would be a tragic injustice to the child to let this window of opportunity close due to his mother's untreated Postpartum Depression.

Each stage in childhood has unique developmental needs. How can the needs of older siblings, whether at a pre-school, school age, or adolescent stage, be affected by a mother suffering from PPD? What would be a red flag for concern in each age group?

The needs of the older siblings should not be overlooked. They, too, need their mother's love and attention and a stable, non-chaotic home environment. If they don't receive this, they may subconsciously react by displaying "attention-seeking behaviors" to compensate for what they are lacking in their home environment. I will attempt to identify the most common behaviors seen in each respective age group.

Pre-school age: regression, immature behavior, wetting/soiling accidents, social withdrawal at home and at school, mood swings

School age: aggression, anxiety disorders, psychosomatic complaints (e.g. stomachaches, headaches, malaise, vague symptoms, etc.)

Adolescent: anti-social behavior, drug and alcohol abuse, depression

The above psychosocial problems can easily mimic academic and neurological issues. The child may be seen as unfocused, hyper, disorganized, and/or struggling with academic issues. Learning disabilities and/or neurological issues may be suspected when in fact the problem is psychosocial in nature and can be effectively reversed as soon as the home environment improves.

༄ྀ

If a woman chooses to use medication for the treatment of PPD, is it safe for her to continue breastfeeding? If

so, which medications would be recommended that are safe for the baby? Does the medication have to be taken in a timed manner to prevent high levels from entering the milk supply during a baby's feeding time?

In my practice, I have seen many moms breastfeed successfully while taking Zoloft for PPD and related disorders. I am sure that there are other anti-depressant and anti-anxiety medications that can be used; this must be discussed with the mother's primary physician. There is an excellent book on breastfeeding and medication called *Medications and Mother's Milk* by Thomas W. Hale PH.D. In this book, medications are classified as L1, L2, etc. These classifications indicate the medications that are safe to use while breastfeeding, having either no side effects or very minimal ones which cannot harm the baby. Consequentially, if these medications are used, there is no need to time feedings (i.e. pump and then discard milk).

Dosages should be supervised by the mother's physician, who should be informed that she is breastfeeding. Under no circumstances should a woman use non-FDA-approved herbal treatments without consulting her physician first.

What side effects may the baby have? Does the baby require medical tests to monitor the level of medication in his system?

As mentioned above, I have not seen any side effects in my pediatric patients whose mothers took Zoloft while breastfeeding. No medical tests were required either. For all other medications, one should read up on the current literature and consult with her doctor.

If a mother wishes to stop taking medication while she is still breastfeeding, will the baby suffer from withdrawal symptoms? If so, what can be done to prevent this?

Medication should be administered under a physician's guidance. If it is done in this manner, the baby should be fine.

☙ ❧

Studies have shown that baby formula is inferior in quality to breast milk. In view of this, many women who feel uncomfortable nursing their baby while taking medication will not seek help for PPD in order that they can continue nursing their baby and know that their baby is receiving the greatest nutritional advantage. What is your opinion on this?

The obligation of the mother is to create a nurturing environment for the child and to feed her child so that he or she can medically thrive, i.e. gain weight. While breast milk is the ideal food for a newborn, a mother must be pragmatic in her approach when deciding how to feed her child.

If one can breastfeed without difficulty, whether taking medication to treat PPD or not, that is fine. If a woman chooses to bottle-feed her child while she is on medication, as she feels that taking medication will cause her increased anxiety and hinder the nurturing process, that is fine, too. Another reason why a woman may choose not to breastfeed is due to a lack of success with it, which can occur even with the help of a lactation consultant.

There is no room for guilt as long as the mother is feeding her child in a comfortable environment that is conducive for proper bonding and nurturing. The mom should feel proud and accomplished to watch her child grow, whether through breastfeeding or formula feeding. Again, I reiterate that there should be **no room for guilt** as long as the mother has made an honest decision, which is ultimately in the best interest of her child.

Today's formulas, while not a perfect match to breast milk, are nutritionally very sound. Ultimately, it is the proper bonding and nurturing between mother and child that will help the baby progress in all areas and help him achieve his potential.

A pediatrician is the main medical professional that most women see during their baby's first year. Are pediatricians trained to spot PPD in new mothers? Would it be appropriate to ask a pediatrician for direction and contact info?

Pediatricians may not be trained to spot PPD. Pediatricians will usually detect something amiss if the mother's affect is obviously flat, or if she appears extremely agitated.

Mothers should not assume that doctors could read their minds. If a mother is suffering from PPD and is looking for guidance, she should take the initiative and ask for help. Although pediatricians are not trained to treat PPD, they can be helpful in directing a new mom to a PPD hotline or support group, or they can discuss other options with her. Another person one can seek more detailed guidance from is the mother's OB-GYN or primary care physician. It is incumbent upon the mother to make the first move for the sake of her child.

Do new mothers feel uncomfortable discussing possible PPD and its effects on the baby with you?

I have found in my practice that patients' mothers with whom I have a good rapport feel comfortable confiding in me about most issues, including Postpartum Depression.

There is no reason for a woman to feel ashamed to speak to a physician. PPD is **not** a reflection of poor character or parenting skills. One should not hesitate to reach out for guidance.

☙ ❧

"Colic is directly linked to a mother's emotional state (and, if present, is therefore the mother's fault)." Is this a myth or fact?

Colic does not have a clear-cut cause. It is assumed to be related to the baby having an immature digestive system, which may cause abdominal spasms. It is a maturational issue which all babies eventually outgrow.

However, although colic is not caused by a mother who is suffering from PPD, the condition can be exacerbated by stress in the home. Therefore, an anxious mother or caretaker can cause the colic symptoms to escalate.

Mothers who are suffering from PPD and who have colicky babies should realize it is crucial for them to have extra help during this stressful time. Otherwise, both the baby's and mother's conditions may worsen and lead to a vicious cycle that is hard to break.

☙ ❧

What message would you give to someone reading this book who thinks that she may be suffering from PPD?

Do not hesitate to seek intervention immediately. It is your obligation to yourself and to your baby.

Resources and Contact Information

Postpartum Support International - A nonprofit organization which provides resources and information about PPD through volunteer coordinators and their website.
www.postpartum.net
Support hotline: (800) 944-4PPD
Office telephone: (503) 849-9453
E-mail: support@postpartum.net

Postpartum Progress- A widely read, responsible blog which provides peer to peer support
www.postpartumprogress.com

Med Ed PPD - A professional education, peer reviewed website with the objective to: A. Further educate and spread awareness among healthcare professionals who may come in contact with women suffering from PPD. B. Provide up to date information for women with PPD and their family and friends.
www.mededppd.org

Midwest Center for Stress and Anxiety (Attacking Anxiety and Depression Program)
P.O. Box 205
Oak Harbor, OH, 43449
Tel: (866) 955-6027
Website: www.stresscenter.com

Books on PPD and Related Disorders:

Freedom from Obsessive Compulsive Disorder (Berkley Books, 2003)
By: Dr. Jonathan Grayson Ph.D

Stop Obsessing (Bantam Books, 2001)
By: Dr. Edna Foa Ph.D

From Panic to Power (Harper Collins, 1996)
By: Lucinda Basset-CEO Midwest Center for Stress and Anxiety

Down Came the Rain (Hyperion, 2005)
By: Brooke Shields

This Isn't What I Expected (Bantam Books, 1994)
By: Karen R. Kleinman MSW and Valerie D. Raskin M.D.

Beyond the Blues (Moodswings Press, 2010)
By: Shoshana S. Bennett PH.D. and Pec Indman, Ed.D., MFT

www.ingramcontent.com/pod-product-compliance
Lightning Source LLC
Chambersburg PA
CBHW071712090426
42738CB00009B/1748